HOPE IS NOT A STRATEGY

Simple Solutions for Doing Business

in the 21st Century

Ted Gee

First published by Dog Ear Publishing
4010 W. 86th Street, Ste H
Indianapolis, IN 46268
www.dogearpublishing.net

ISBN: 978-159858-767-8

This book is printed on acid-free paper.

Printed in the United States of America

Dedication

I would like to dedicate this book to my late mother, Mary Coley, and the late Nathan Lyons, Shirkey Gee, and Steven Jordan.

TABLE OF CONTENTS

Dedication iii
Acknowledgements vii
Introduction ix
Preface xi

LEADERSHIP 1
   WHO IS IN CHARGE 2
   DEFINING LEADERSHIP 7
   FINDING AND TRAINING LEADERS 12
   TIME/GRADE AND THE SILVER BULLET 14
   THE LEVELS & ROLES OF LEADERSHIP 20
   LEADERSHIP AND PROCESS 27

The Organizational Journey 41
   VISION/MISSION 43
   STRATEGY 45
   CURRENT STATE OF THE BUSINESS 55
   SYSTEMS 72
   3-YEAR STRATEGY MATRIX PROCESS 76
   INSTITUTING CHANGE 83
   THE BUSINESS OPERATING SYSTEM 85
   AFTER ACTION REVIEW 100
   COMMUNICATIONS 107
   PUTTING IT ALL TOGETHER 112

Appendix 117
   SIX SIGMA ACRONYMS 118
   LEAN ENTERPRISE 122
   LEAN DEFINITIONS OR ACRONYMS 123
   LEAN METHODOLOGIES 125
   LEAN TOOLS 126
   LEAN FORMULAS OR CALCULATIONS 131
   STRATEGY MATRIX 133
   ROAD MAP 134
   30, 60, 90 DAY PLAN 135
   COMMUNICATIONS PLAN 136
   END NOTES 137

Acknowledgements

A special thanks to Ted Sr, Gladys, Carmalinda and the boys.

I would also like to thank those that have been a great help to me personally (Lucille Potts, Gene and Tyna Walker, LTC Robert Reese, Darlene Barr, Ken and Janet Foggs, Carl Sharperson, Allison Judge, The Davis', Billie Osborne, Todd Lee, Pam Jewell, Belinda Artis, Cindi Adams, Tyrone Hilliard, Chance McCall, Barry and Jocelyn Armstrong, and many, many other family and friends.)

I have been blessed with many professional mentors who have had played key roles in helping to steer me in the right direction and away from career-ending ditches. I would like to thank all of those who played these roles professionally (MSG Herman Taylor, Avia Toney, John Adams, Darryl Littleton, Mike Mueller, Todd Lee, Brian Smith, Jeff Bleustein, Tim Zetwick, Ron Hutchinson, Mike Heerhold, Jerome Johnson, Dave Bozeman, the late Jim Threatt and many others).

I would also like to thank LTG Marvin Covault (ret), for his input and contributions to this book.

Many of the tough love lessons that I learned at home resulted in me driving forward without seeking an external lifeline to fall back on. It forced me to seek out solutions and not make excuses for why things could not get done.

Introduction

I am writing this book because as we continue to look at a once-strong economy decline, healthcare costs escalate, an education system that seems to be getting left behind, and a government that seems to be watching a different channel than the American people, I want to help find solutions. As many companies and businesses focus on leaving the US, moving to other countries to get lower cost labor, and as Wall Street continues to force companies to run organizations from the unrealistic perspective of short-term results, almost playing a game of hot potato, I want to help find solutions.

I believe that if we look at the root cause of the issues and not the symptoms, then focus on fixing these, we can become more competitive and will be better equipped to continue having great success and again be the land of opportunity. I believe that by understanding the root cause of how much goods and services actually cost, utilizing processes instead of outdated financial practices, the people in leadership positions will be better equipped to make sound decisions. We will be able to truly understand the cost of healthcare and provide a solution that benefits all. We will be able to fix the educational system, and help people achieve their dreams of greater prosperity. I believe that the government needs a significant facelift, an efficiency overhaul. I believe that the foundation for solving these issues is to understand leadership and the requirements of that role, understanding the current state of an organization, defining where it wants to go and developing a solid plan to get there. There needs to be a lot more accountability and commitment in our organizations, outside of high salaries and big bonuses for short-term results. In the words of Dr. Martin Luther King Jr., "there is a need for fierce urgency now!" Urgency in our entire country, we must do something now, or many people will not be able to afford the products and services being imported into our country! Affordable healthcare, effective education and the American Dream may be slipping away.

This book will provide a framework and introduce and discuss new processes to help almost any company meet the challenges of a global economy and reverse or avoid the pitfalls inherent with outmoded management paradigms. I want to paint a simple picture on how to be successful in business utilizing leadership and process. This book will provide those in leadership positions with an opportunity to understand what it is they are responsible for, and a method for actually solving the problems they face. This is a recipe for "how to's", which can be of great value. I also want to provide an opportunity for those looking to start a business, large or small, to acquire some important tools for developing a solid strategy and process management at the outset. I believe that defining the roles of leaders, and having some actual process tools for running a business, will help all to become more successful, and may help to save many of our businesses. Success for all readers will be based on understanding the game and hard work. This book will cover understanding the game by focusing on leadership and process. The hard work will be up to you.

I have had a wonderful career, first as an officer in the military, then rising to the executive ranks in corporate America. I have worked my way from frontline supervisor to have been at the Chief Operating Officer, President, Vice President and Director level. I am an ordinary person, frail and flawed, that has had extraordinary opportunities to prove myself. I have had to work extremely hard to actually learn the tasks that have led to my successes. I have had the opportunity to work with some great companies such as Corning, FMC, Harley Davidson Motor Company, Pulte Homes, and Ingersoll Rand, where I gained much of my experiences. These opportunities have been a series of learned experiences and timely opportunities to execute successes during times of major business need or while on a burning platform.

This book will allow the reader to understand the details required in setting strategies, being a leader, and executing processes. You will be challenged to look at your organization as it is, rather than what you wish it to be. If you are starting a new business, you will be required to plan your business with the level of detail that will ensure that there is a clear strategy, people are in alignment, and the processes will support your financials. If you are running a business from the finance office and not processes, I can assure you that predictability and reliability will continue to be a huge challenge for your organization.

Preface

Einstein or the Three Stooges

Do your projects begin as if this man designed them?

And then end up as if they were done by this man
and his two friends?

Have you ever wondered why your organization or an organization that you may have been a part of changes directions so frequently? Have you ever thought that your boss or someone at the top does not have a clue what is going on within the organization? How did that person end up in that management position? How many times have you heard that we need more communication? Who is responsible for training and development? How many times have you thought that your boss knew less about what was going on than you do? How do I progress through the organization faster? Wondered where did those financial numbers come from? What about those metrics? Do we have a strategy or plan? Am I a valued employee? Why some companies are more successful than others, or are they? Are you concerned about the number of jobs being outsourced from the US to low-cost countries? Are you worried about the stock market? I am sure that some of these questions are familiar to you regardless of your profession, whether you are a leader within a fortune 500 company, a small business, religious organization, school teacher, doctor, lawyer, or any other position that has a responsibility of being led, or leading others.

The purpose of this book is to give you, the reader, some tools that are necessary in the success of any business. It will be an opportunity to learn, to understand and, most importantly, to obtain key tools needed to implement "the strategy" or "the plan" for almost any business. We will focus on the level of detail needed to deal with many complex business solutions and ideas throughout any organization. We will look at leadership and the roles and responsibilities of all participants at every level. We will examine the importance of the details of the strategy in every business. This book will also focus on the processes that answer "what, who, why, when, where and how much" that are the basis of the many questions you may face daily. There are many books on the market today that focus on theory, framework and views of what is supposed to happen in businesses for success to occur. There are also quite a few books on the experiences of many successful business leaders and what they did or did not do very well while running their organizations. Very few of the books on the market today are able to provide a clearly defined plan that lays out the "details" required to be successful as a leader! Very few of these books highlight the roadmap successful leaders have followed, or how they have actually landed where they did in the organizations. This book will highlight the synergies required between people, processes and systems to ensure that the businesses are successful.

Many of you are part of companies, businesses, teams, governments, and communities where dependency upon others is paramount to your success. This dependency should be the soul of a successful team, and this team must have a leader! A successful team has great leadership, great people, great strategies, great processes and great systems. A team can function with very bright people, but it will never realize its full potential without strong leadership that can motivate team members to be great. The interdependency of an efficient leader and an effective team is paramount to successes within any business. Without this leadership component, there are often constant changes within the organization, and resulting chaos throughout the ranks. This results in poor financial performance, which in turn results in layoffs, blame games, political finger-pointing, strained relationships, sacrificial lambs, firing and other unproductive energy-draining activities seen in many companies today.

Many people start out with visions, strategies, plans and other ideas that from the outset seem to be the greatest ever invented, but they end up as binders taking up shelf space and collecting dust. How many of us have participated in "strategic planning sessions" that last for days, weeks, and in some instances months, that end up as large documents, containing lots of numbers, and few if any directions as to how these numbers or plans will be executed or implemented. Many of these so called "strategies" are being completed with great fanfare, but questions remain unanswered, such as: What is the voice of the customer? What is the rate the customers want the product or service? What level of quality is expected? How many people will this require? Do we have the experience in-house? What type of training will be required? What processes are working well throughout the company? Which ones are not? Is recruiting in alignment with the strengths and weaknesses of the organization, starting with the leadership?

Many of the questions required in a comprehensive strategy become overshadowed by the financial myopia of the organization.

While the financials should be the predictable end result of the processes and strategies of the business, it is instead the key driver of what, how, and when things will get completed. It is obvious that every organization needs money for operations and must generate revenue to be successful, and there must be effective financial reporting systems in place. However, we must remember that the financials are a result of the process, not the other way around. As many companies continue to outsource products, services, and other key occupations once dominated by a strong economy in the US, for the purpose of "impacting the bottom line," we will continue to lose ground to the rest of the world. If we invested more time fixing our companies where they are now and dealing with root causes of issues, instead of grasping for "Silver Bullets," shifting the blame and the bill to the next watch, or sugar coating the issues, a global economy can be great for our future. Solving the problems and having processes in place to eliminate the waste and deal with problems that arise is the key. We must understand the current state of our business, business unit, function, or area to begin getting a true picture of what is going on, and to begin solving problems.

This book will discuss and address the process of seeing the current state of the business. By understanding the current state, or what the true conditions are, you will be in the position to review the processes and determine the "how to's" to implement the changes that will solve issues.

This book addresses the synergies required between leadership and process tools, such as lean, six sigma, and all of the Silver Bullets being grasped at by many fortune 500 managers. This will be a guide for those interested in running a small business, a large corporation, positions within governments, or even charitable organizations. It is a guide that will help all to understand what is required to be successful, the who, what, why, when, where and how of successful businesses.

As we begin our journey with a discussion of leadership, I am reminded of Lee Iacocca's new book "Where Have all the Leaders Gone?" He explains how this problem can be seen in every facet of our country, and with passion he states: "Am I the only guy in this country who's fed up with what's happening? Where the hell is our outrage? ... We've got a gang of clueless bozos steering our ship of state right over a cliff, we've got corporate gangsters stealing us blind ..." Because this is an issue that is becoming bigger and more urgent, we will look at the problems Iacocca highlights and we will address the 'why' of the problem and then provide concrete steps to understanding what we can do to fix the problem. This will be starting with the basics; what is a leader, what are the roles and responsibilities of leaders, and what it is that you can do. In the subsequent chapters and sections we will look at strategy and the plan of execution so that you can succeed.

LEADERSHIP

You cannot be a leader, and ask other people to follow
you, unless you know how to follow, too.

SAM RAYBURN - former Speaker of the House

WHO IS IN CHARGE

As we begin to look at leadership, its roles and responsibilities, and what leadership truly is, I would like to preface it with the following: I do not believe that leaders are born, they are made. I do believe that people are born with certain instincts and style that can be honed or coupled with great development, and great mentors can provide a huge advantage. Opportunity is also an irreplaceable addition to the equation. You must have the opportunity and when presented with the chance to excel, must be able to recognize and seize the opportunity, whether this opportunity is as a leader in a larger established organization or in an entrepreneurial venture.

Many people think that a manager who crushes unions, ships jobs overseas, or fires people to improve the bottom line are great business people. At least these may be the short-term answers in the minds of some on Wall Street. When profits decline or stocks drop, often the answer is to get rid of people. Get rid of the overhead and that will fix the problem. In some cases I am sure that the overhead in organizations far outweighs the productivity or necessary head count. What about companies that reduce, restructure, layoff, right size, downsize, or whatever terminology they may use for getting rid of people? After this change, outside of the manipulated financials, how often does this result in increased efficiencies? It may address some waste issues; however, are the processes being fixed first? How will one person or a smaller group of people handle the job that was once done by many? Yes, there may be some technology to replace these people, but the technology must be managed in the same sense of completeness as manual processes. There are a number of other questions that must be asked. Are there processes in place that will define the number of people needed to run a particular function? Will the customer's needs be met? Will you be able to deliver the customer's product or service at the time required by the customer, at the quality expected, and the cost they are willing to pay?

Unions

Unions have long held a controlling aspect in many businesses but they are definitely losing their foothold, and in some cases, their usefulness within the United States. This is occurring because of the union leadership's inability to change with the economy. Yes, unions may not be in the same demand or have the same usefulness as many years ago and yes there are low-cost (labor) countries all over the world. What is the answer? The union leaders must keep up with the changing times and the cyclicality of the economy. There is still a need for unions in many cases and the reason is poor leadership within companies! The leadership process for the union leadership is just as important as the need for development and change of other leaders within the company. As a part of good leadership, people should always be the priority. "People first, company always" is a slogan that I have used throughout my career. Without the people in a union or non-union environment the company will not succeed. Without the company, the people or unions will not have a job. In the instances where unions are still in demand, a mutually beneficial relationship will strengthen the longevity of the company during the global competition for jobs.

When you think about the purpose of unions in the US, the reasons were clear (work conditions, unfair treatment of workers, fair pay, accountability, benefits, etc). The root cause for the rise of labor unions was poor leadership within companies! There are many companies that have done a great job at addressing many of the issues surrounding the original need for unions. Harley Davidson has not only done a great job with its relationships with unions, but has become known worldwide for its joint leadership philosophy. The relationship between Harley Davidson and its unions has been a huge part of the turnaround success at Harley Davidson. The company understood the value of all of its employees, and has spent enormous amounts of time and money on educating the workforce on the big picture and the value of all of its employees. This commitment was in large part nothing more than defining and holding management accountable to the roles and responsibilities of strong leadership. There are some other companies that have done well with their relationships with unions, but not in staggering numbers. Fortunately, or unfortunately, there is still a need for unions in many parts of our country, and the reason continues to be poor leadership! Some of the same reasons that were foundations for the union movement many years ago remain (work conditions, unfair treatment of workers, fair pay, accountability and benefits).

Competition
It is ironic that as the shift to a global economy accelerates, the forces that generate competition are taking control of our organizations. The result of this change in focus is that the search for the low-cost labor countries continues to allow our businesses to remain competitive. A little more than 10 years ago, Mexico was the place that many of our companies relocated to for low-cost labor. It was the place to go for saving money in labor costs and increasing the bottom line. After Mexico, China was the place to go to save money. India, Vietnam and other countries are now becoming hotbeds for low-cost labor and moving many jobs. Like Mexico, we have found out that the labor cost savings there and in China have often been offset by the poor quality of products and the additional logistics cost. As we look at the number of products coming back into the US because of quality issues, safety issues, and other issues, the cost savings are being severely diluted. The primary root cause of why we are not competitive in the manufacturing and service industries today can be addressed with a familiar theme, and that is poor leadership! As we look to the lower-cost countries to solve our problems, we will have an economy that will not be able to afford the low-cost products being brought back into the US.

Wall Street
If Wall Street continues to ask those that are running businesses how much money they will generate, and not ask to see the strategies or plans that will support them, we will continue to have issues such as Enron, Tyco, and all of the other companies cooking the books. One of the major questions we must begin to address is WHY our leaders cannot make our businesses more competitive and look to offset labor costs through efficiencies and keep jobs in the US. We cannot continue to run businesses by making the financials

fit the questions being driven by the analysts on Wall Street. If Wall Street is demanding certain percentages of returns from companies, then they must also begin to ask how the results will be obtained. If the company commits to a 15% return by increasing production 25% and sales 20%, then how will this be achieved, must be the subsequent question. These questions will drive additional questions. If your plants are only running at 20% effectiveness, and you are not addressing the plant issues, then it is highly unlikely that you will increase volume 25% without incurring tremendous expansion costs. This is a leadership issue. In the same manner, just reducing headcount and not addressing the process issues will not solve the problem long term. It will not matter that you can have better labor cost in India, Vietnam, or any other low-cost areas if the leadership competencies domestically are not addressed. If the US-based company is not operating efficiently in the US, moving the product or service overseas, where logically you will need more people that can help train, develop, and build the processes that will supposedly help you reach your returns, is only a band-aid. It is clearly the responsibility of the leadership in all organizations to have strategies and plans, to work to enhance the effectiveness of the organization, and look to increase profits for the long term rather than just quarterly. This responsibility includes clear accountability within every facet of the organization, Sales, Engineering, Operations, Customer Service, Aftermarket, and all of the transactional areas, Human Resources, Finance, Legal, and Information Technologies.

Wall Street has a clear objective of driving the profitability of the financial markets, but it can better achieve this by improving the level of due diligence the analysts perform on companies that we invest in. This change alone would have helped to avoid the over-inflation of the ratings that occurred with the failed dot com boom, and has been apparent in the current housing market, and has expressed itself in the values implied to the lenders of subprime mortgages. The failure of Wall Street to properly assess value has led to the current trend where private equity firms are purchasing distressed or failing companies for pennies on the dollar.

With the focus of private equity companies on making money for their investors, there are three primary strategies employed. At times the objectives will be to transform the companies and hold them for a few years and either take them public or sell them for a sizeable gain. There will also be those entities that will want to keep the companies for long term. Unfortunately, there are private equity companies that are more focused on leveraging the remaining assets of the distressed company and capitalizing on the monthly interest payments for generating profits. This lack of interest in truly fixing the distressed companies will continue to exacerbate the downward spiral of many companies and add to the number of lost jobs. I expect that we will be hearing a great deal about the successes and failures of the continually growing number of private equity companies in the coming years and their impact on businesses since a growing number of these groups are being formed for the sole purpose of making money without the constraints imposed on public companies.

DEFINING LEADERSHIP

Before, we begin to address the leadership issue, I wanted to identify a problem that we can all relate to: understanding exactly what it is that we are trying to deal with. If we are to begin to explore the roles and responsibilities of leadership in an organization, it is imperative that we understand the differences between the terms, Leadership and Management, which are often used interchangeably. For communications to be effective everyone has to be on the same page and be in agreement as to what the words we are using actually mean. So here comes the English lesson.

Definitions of Leadership and Management

Definitions are from:

- Webster's New International Dictionary, Second Edition, 1946, unabridged
- Webster's Third New international Dictionary, 1993
- Wikipedia, the Free Encyclopedia, 3/13/08

Manage: comes from the Italian "menagerie," to train (a horse), to exercise in graceful or skillful action, to put through his paces.

-ment: can mean
  1. Concrete result or means (fulfillment)
  2. Action
  3. State or quality

Management: the judicious use of means to accomplish an end; the act, art, capacity, or skill, tact or cleverness, the actions taken to get things done.

Mary Parker Follett (1868–1933) defined Management as "the act of getting things done through people." Follett suggested that organizations function on the principle of power "with" and not power "over."

Management is generally a multi-step process:

- Assessment
- Planning
- Control

    or

- Planning
- Organizing
- Leading
- Coordinating
- Controlling

Leader: a person… that goes before to guide and show the way… who proceeds or directs in some action, opinion, or movement.

-ship: denotes the state, condition, or quality, the art or skill.

In any educational or training process, one comes face to face with the challenges of language and the oft times confused meanings of words and terms used. Such is the case in the discussion of **Leadership** and **Management**. Although these words are often used interchangeably in business circles, we believe that they need to be separate and distinct.

Leadership denotes the quality or skill of a person that goes before, who proceeds, to guide and show the way in some action, movement, or opinion. As our definition is expanded you will see that effective leadership involves the ability to act with initiative.

Management is the action or process taken to get things done; it implies the judicious use of means to accomplish an end. That includes;
- Assessment
- Planning
- Organizing
- Leading
- Coordinating
- Controlling

The primary distinction between leadership and management is that one is a state of being while the other denotes actions engaged in. But, they are also intimately associated. A leader needs to have solid management skills so that there can be reasonable confidence that the direction he or she is taking the organization is correct and achievable. A manager who is involved in "the act of getting things done through people" will ultimately be more effective if he or she possesses leadership skills.

These two terms and concepts have clearly different roles within an organization. As we look at organizations and the account-ability within these organizations, everything must begin with the leader! Although, the roles of leaders and managers are different, it is important to remember that all leaders must have management skills, but not all managers have leadership skills. That is not to say that some managers cannot become leaders, because I believe that they can. With good training, development and good instincts, some managers may become effective in leadership roles, but definitely not all. It is also important to know that at different levels of the orga-nization, the roles and responsibilities of each are different, and there has been very little focus on where leaders come from, how they are trained, and what is expected of them.

While virtually everyone in a leadership role seeks the respect that comes from the position of power, respect is earned and lasting accolades come from accomplishments. There is clearly a dif-ference between a true leader, one who is skilled in the art of leader-ship and has a proven background of success, and those in leadership positions because of relationships, or time and grade. There are examples of individuals that were very bright and great motivators of people that have had successes in leadership roles, but in most of these cases there have not been any provision made for developing a continuum of leadership and the organization falls in to decline when that leader is no longer on the scene. It is this training and nurturing of the leadership mentality that needs to be addressed in American business.

In an effort to deal with this deficiency, there are many books on the market today that discuss leadership, the traits of a successful leader, and what a leader should be doing. There are also some courses on leadership available, but not many organizations focus on leadership as a learning process. The United States military is one of the few organizations in the world that truly focuses on leadership. Because of this, there are many companies that try to recruit and capitalize on this rare skill called leadership.

A leader in the military has a responsibility for the health, welfare, and lives of their troops while achieving the objectives dictated by the strategy. In the business world, leaders have the responsibility for the livelihoods of their employees, while maximizing the business operation for shareholder value. "A leader is not synonymous with power. Being in a position of power does not automatically qualify that person as a leader. Holding a position of power has decision authority over, subordinates, issues and operating procedures. In addition, this person must also have the ability to communicate a vision of an end state throughout the organization, so a vision can be eventually executed. Effective leadership does not require that every detail be thought through before decisions are made or programs launched. Seeking that last bit of information rather than going with your gut can paralyze an organization, and in fact increase risk by missing the most opportune time to move forward. The challenge is to get the large issues in focus and ensure everyone on the project is working toward the same end state and then move toward execution." (Lt. General Marvin Covault, Ret.).

It does not matter whether you are leading in the military, the corporate world; government or a fast food restaurant, the art of leadership is the same. The responsibilities are the same, and the expectation to lead your employees, partner with your suppliers, the community, and often the government, are the same. Most importantly, the responsibilities of meeting or exceeding your customer's expectations are always the same.

In this chapter we will look at some of the questions that naturally arise when you begin to think about leadership and provide some clarity.

1. Where do leaders come from?
2. How are they trained?
3. Are there any universities that train leaders to lead? Is leadership learned or innate?
4. What are the roles and responsibilities of leaders at different levels of the workplace?

What are the differences between leaders and managers?

FINDING AND TRAINING LEADERS

The US Military has one of the most comprehensive training programs in the world for its leaders. Its officers go through a variety of methods of intense leadership training, whether from the Military Academies, the ROTC (Reserved Officer Training Corps) program or OCS (Officer Candidate School). There are many other courses structured for non commissioned officers that provide much of the same foundation for leading. This training takes years and, as a person progresses to another rank or sometimes jobs in their military career, they have to go through additional training. This additional training will help them to be successful at the next level and next job the military personnel are moving into. This training helps to ensure that the people have the tools and foundation of knowledge for making decisions in most situations, thereby hopefully avoiding the dreaded Peter Principal. Much of the role of a leader in the military is to provide a vision or strategy, and then train and develop those under their command to be able to execute their jobs effectively and to protect lives. Some of this is instinct, and it is the instinct factor that separates out the great leaders. But to focus on this is to lose the focus on achieving results in our organizations. Great leaders are rare and even good leaders are few and far between.

I am not suggesting that all those who complete the training in the US Military are great leaders, merely that they do come equipped with the tools to be successful under responsibilities that they may have or conditions that they may face in leading an organization at a level commensurate with their experience. There are other methods of learning leadership tools besides joining the Army or hiring someone with military command experience, such as The Center for Creative Leadership, located in Greensboro, NC. The Center has other sites in the US and around the globe that may be more accessible for your organization. There are organizations such as the American Management Association and others that have classes or seminars that focus on leadership and management tools, and quite a few reputable organizations that can help with leadership assessments, 360 feedback, and individual development plans for those in leadership positions as well. These organizations focus on helping people in leadership roles become more effective. Many of these organizations are based on the psychology of leadership and seek to develop their individual development plans based on statistics, probability and theories. They are not generally geared for the initial preparation of an individual for a life as a leader or their roles and responsibilities throughout the continuum. I have had the opportunity to work with a few of these organizations across the country. I am sure that there are plenty of other organizations that may be of help to some leaders; however, I'm not sure any of them provide the time and focus on the art of leadership as a process continuum as does the US Military.

There are great institutions of higher learning throughout the US that have excellent curriculums at the undergraduate and graduate levels. Many of these are great Ivy League Schools, most are not. And some much smaller schools are geared toward providing the best business people, lawyers, doctors, teachers, and so on in the world. Although many of these schools have great teaching about the philosophy and fundamentals of business and use case studies, they are not teaching leadership in a developmental method that would make those in leadership positions more effective. This would ultimately make many companies and businesses more successful. You could finish at the top of your class in Business from your university; or Magna Cum Laude at Harvard Business School, or come from a wealthy family, and still be a terrible leader. As many schools in our educational system continue to focus on *what* to think, and not *how* to think, presenting case studies and other historical modus operandi as methods of teaching business leadership will have very little impact. Other than the fact that most great leaders are bright, there seems to be little connection between education or intelligence and leadership skills, and no guarantee that bright people will be great leaders. Those that are in the medical field learn about healthcare, teachers learn about education, and engineers learn about engineering, and very little of their developmental focus is on leadership. Unless they begin to provide specific training on the subject of leadership, organizations are going to need to look elsewhere.

TIME IN GRADE AND THE SILVER BULLET

After careful analysis it can be seen that in corporate America there are adequate systems in place to train managers, but for the most part there is no real understanding of what is required for leadership, and there are very few programs to build and develop leaders. Instead, businesses have relied on luck and hope, which have their expression in time in grade or Silver Bullets, to provide the steady stream of future leaders.

Time in grade

Time in grade is a term frequently used in the government and union environments. It is a system that ensures people do not develop or move faster than their time in service warrants. In many organizations people are not promoted based on competencies, they move through organizations only after they have been in an organization or a position for a specified time or, in some instances, have checked certain boxes of perceived accomplishments. In the military, time and grade is coupled with certain competencies and requirements for development. If the requirements or training are not accomplished, the military personnel normally will not be promoted. This process is also used to weed out or eliminate people who are not capable or able to move to the next level or rank. This addresses the issue of people being retired in jobs because of tenure. In the military, you move up or out. In many organizations, people remain in positions for many years, often resting on their past successes. Sometimes these people are not being very productive or supportive to the long-term strategy. This can be detrimental when you have diamonds in the rough or potential superstars in the lower ranks that have the skill sets required to support the long-term strategy or success of the organization. Often these people do not move up fast enough, and can get bored and leave organizations for a better challenge.

My first position out of the military was with Corning Inc as a front line supervisor. It was a great experience and I had some great successes turning around my first manufacturing operation. Without much direction or guidance, I helped to develop some of the divisions first High Performance Work Teams, and they yielded some tremendous results. High Performance Work Teams are a hope of many companies today. They are also great in concept; however, they require a tremendous amount of training, development and involvement in the big picture of the company. There is a tremendous amount of trust required in these environments because of the amount of information that is shared. In this role, I trained all of my teams on the big picture and developed an effective cross training model that allowed a great deal of flexibility within the operation. This type of training enabled the employees to be involved with daily decisions and idea generation that helped the overall efficiency of the operation. Because of this involvement there were significant performance increases in delivery, quality, and a reduction of cost. The impact was noticed by the plant leadership, the unions, and most surprisingly, some senior executives from the CEO staff at corporate. These successes were rewarded by a promotion (to another troubled area of the company in a different division). This was another huge turnaround opportunity that involved a multitude of issues. Although this promotion was greatly appreciated, I had a sense of nervousness and concern because I was not sure that I had learned enough in my first role to be as successful in this second role. There was virtually no teaching or preparation for this added responsibility, which was unlike what I had experienced in my military service. There was no strategy or plan, other than short-sighted production requirements that I was asked to fulfill, and many of the processes that were in place had been developed years before my arrival and continued to be used without considering if they were truly effective. In an effort to do the best job possible, I attended all the management, supervisory, and technical training that was available during my time at Corning. While most of the training I attended lasted a few hours per class or session and were helpful, most of the successes I was experiencing could be correlated with what I had learned through the leadership skills gained in the military, team athletics, and a good deal of common sense. Many of my successes came from understanding what was going on within the people and processes and being able to effectively communicate. We developed some daily meetings with the shop floor employees where we discussed what the expectations

were, how they thought we were to achieve the goals, and what barriers existed. We also instituted accountability within the processes
by developing operational matrics and communicating the big picture to the employees. We developed cross training programs and
broke many production records. Nothing really earth-shattering was
implemented; however, the combined effect of these small changes
seemed to be effective and received a great deal of attention throughout the organization. This was very different than the military
because there we had leadership training, and training and preparation for new roles was always provided. This was my first real experience with time in grade, and the Silver Bullet, and in this case I was
management's Silver Bullet, and advancement was normally predicated on time and grade.

I was recruited from Corning to a position with greater
responsibility at FMC. During the interview process, I was assured
that there was a better succession planning process, and I would get
the tools necessary for my career growth. My assignment at FMC
was a turnaround opportunity with the expectation of implementing
a more effective High Performance Work Environment. This turned
out to be very similar to my role at Corning. I had tremendous successes improving the overall efficiencies of the business segment by
utilizing leadership, improving the processes, and engaging the people. Again, I learned about time in grade, and the Silver Bullet. Prior
to my arrival, there was not a known strategic plan, a few sporadic
metrics, limited communication with the employees, and no succession plan in place for developing leaders. There was a financial plan
in place and that is what drove the business. The processes there were
archaic and were able to be changed to become more efficient with
the help of the newly engaged employees. I did not see the sophistication of leadership, nor the systems that I was expecting and had
learned from the military.

After a few years at FMC, I was recruited by Harley Davidson Motor Company. Although I was becoming somewhat disillu-
sioned with my experiences in corporate America, it appeared that I
was doing well and adding value to the companies I worked for. I was
very concerned that although my career was going well and I had
taken many courses at both companies, I still did not notice the structure of leadership or the level of accountability and commitment that

was customary in the military. Harley Davidson turned out to have some different circumstances, with the turnaround of the company from the brink of bankruptcy and backlog of motorcycles being key drivers. There was a tremendous amount of commitment by virtually all of the employees throughout the company. The levels of communication and involvement made the required change and turnaround fun. I have been able to transition to different companies with different products, because of my leadership skills and eagerness to learn; building motorcycles was no different.

Just like my previous stops, I had the opportunity to achieve some major successes at Harley Davidson. Because of their stronger leadership and more open environment, I took a different approach to my concern for learning and understanding the leadership development process. After providing some major accomplishments with the new worldwide distribution center, I approached my boss with an innocent but pointed question, "Can you help me to learn more about business?" He had been a great mentor and had helped me to understand corporate America, more than I had learned in all my previous positions combined. He understood the responsibility of training and development of subordinates, which was truly refreshing. He responded favorably and asked me to tell him what I needed to know and he would help. Although I appreciated the response, I was looking for a different answer. I was looking for guidance on what I needed to learn and know. I was at the point of realizing there was a lot I did not know, but I wasn't sure what it was that I didn't know. So I asked if he would be ok if I were to visit his boss for some mentoring? He welcomed the suggestion and, as always, supported my eagerness to develop professionally. What I was looking for was someone to help me to understand more about the roles and responsibilities of the leadership continuum. As confident as I was, what I was trying to understand was more about the things that I did not know as a leader, which would prepare me for future roles.

I continued my pilgrimage up through the chain of command, to the senior VP level, always with positive encouraging responses but no real information. At this point, I was wondering if I would be able to learn more about the roles and responsibilities of leadership needed in higher levels of responsibility throughout the company, or whether it was a time in grade scenario that I was facing. After a couple of weeks of self reflection, with great curiosity I decided to approach the CEO of Harley Davidson, Jeff Bleustein, to get his perspective on the training and development of leaders. With his open door policy, I scheduled an appointment with him to discuss what I might do to continue developing in my career to progress to a more senior level within the organization. Although my initial question for him was asked in a different manner and with the same focus, he understood the intent. My question to him was, "What did he do differently to get promoted to the level and position that he was at, than some of the other vice presidents in the organization that were of a similar age?" Since I had just helped to rebuild the worldwide distribution network, I wondered what developmental preparation and path I could take that would help me to make larger, more responsible decisions with more accountability. What would prepare me for senior leadership? He understood my requests and, in addition to responding favorably, he agreed to see me periodically as a mentor. After some additional dialogue with Jeff Bleustein, and reassurance that I had gotten support from the chain of command, I continued my operational initiatives. I realized that with all the great things about and happening at Harley Davidson, there was no system in place to allow for individual growth outside of the time in grade scenario.

Silver Bullets
In addition to the use of time in grade to provide for solutions to the leadership problem, many organizations fall into the trap of seeking Silver Bullets. A Silver Bullets is a metaphor for a simple remedy for a difficult or intractable problem, a solution believed to be totally effective. It is a reference to the folklore belief that such bullets are the only weapons which can kill a werewolf. As mentioned earlier, at Corning, the senior management was using the "if someone does an excellent job, promote them" Silver Bullet. Other common Silver Bullet solutions to the leadership continuum problem are:

- Hire JMOs (Junior Military Officers). This certainly provides a pool of people who have had leadership training, but as I found out, it does not provide continued support and developmental training needed to establish a continuum.

- Hire a Harvard (or your favorite school) MBA. Again, you may have an excellent person with a great education, and they may be well trained for the job at hand, but will they be just as competent and well prepared when they feel they are ready for a promotion?
- In the same vein as hiring an MBA, many companies hire in a leader who has done a similar job at another company. The problem comes in not understanding how much of their success was attributable to circumstances and how much was a result of their leadership abilities.
- Implement a software solution like SAP with the expectation that it will allow the existing leadership structure to operate in a more effective manner.

Like most endeavors in life, there is a lot of time and money spent trying the quick and painless way to solve problems. Developing leaders is no different. The only real solution is to make a commitment to the long view and begin developing a culture of leadership, starting with you. So, let's get started.

THE LEVELS & ROLES OF LEADERSHIP

It is clear and learned in the military that there are different levels of leadership. At these different levels of leadership, the roles and responsibilities of its leaders are clearly different. Lt. General Marvin Covault, Ret. wrote in his book, "From Vision to Execution," that "Leaders at different levels in an organization do not perform the same functions differently; leaders at different levels perform different functions." The Leadership continuum consists of three different functions, which are defined as the Strategic Level, Operational Level, and Direct or Tactical Level. This is very important as we look at what is commonly referred to as the Peter Principle. This is where a person at the direct/tactical level of leadership is promoted based on the successes they have had at that level, without receiving the requisite training needed for the increased responsibilities and different functions of the higher level. Although the functions are different at the other levels, they are expected to perform the same. When they fail, rarely is the focus on the different functions and skills required, but the person's failure to perform. This is very unfortunate but happens in a variety of venues. "From Vision to Execution" makes the point that all leadership levels have some elements in common. For example, every leader processes information and turns it into knowledge. Also, all leaders need to be thinkers and analysts; and given a certain amount of information they turn it into solutions. They do this by assessing alternatives based on incomplete data and choosing a course of action. This is commonly referred to as decision-making. **All leaders are decision makers.**

Covault also states, "Another element all three levels have in common is generating support. There is always more than one course of action to achieve a goal; you, the leader, decide which method the team is going to use. Influencing people, gaining consensus and generating support is a continuous function at every level. While all leadership levels share some common challenges they, of course differ by degree. For example, decisions at the strategic level affect more people than do the direct leader's decisions. A CEO's pronouncement commits more resources in manpower, time and materials and has a wider consequence than those of his or her subordinate leaders."

I believe that there is a definable role and responsibility at every level of every organization, and it is not much difference in scope than in the military. This delineation of roles and responsibilities can be of great help to every leader, as it allows them to not only understand the roles, but it helps with succession planning and, most importantly, training and development of subordinates throughout the organization. Understanding the roles and responsibilities within an organization, and its strength and weaknesses, should be the prerequisite for any staffing needs for a successful organization. The correlation of Strategic, Operational, and Tactical could reflect a sense of order within any organization. It will also help to define the roles and responsibilities for those individuals at each level.

As we have stated, the three different functions are the Strategic Level, Operational Level, and Direct or Tactical Levels. This is called the "leadership continuum," and the responsibilities of these functions are:

Strategic Level of Leadership

This is the senior level of leadership that, depending on the size of the organization, is where the C-Level (chairman), presidents, vice presidents, and some directors are housed. They are clearly responsible for the vision, mission and strategy of the organization. The onus of completing the entire strategy or holistic strategy is held at this level. After the vision, mission and strategy are completed, this level is responsible for ensuring that the communication is communicated to every employee. They are also responsible for ensuring that there are metrics tied to the strategy to which all employees are held accountable. The metrics should be in a common format and cascaded down throughout the organization. As the metrics fall into alignment, they should be translated with the appropriate accountability of every level and every function. The vision and mission should be a clear view of where the organization is going. The strategy should incorporate how things are going to get done to support the vision. The strategy should include voice of the customer, competition, integrated metrics for every function within the organization, aligned to the vision/strategy, a delivery mechanism (Sales,

Inventory, and Operations Planning [SIOP] process to understand deliveries), succession planning, and a recruiting plan equipped with training and developmental requirements at all levels. This strategy should include a financial plan that is a result of the organization's business processes and how to's, or a plan of execution across the organization. There should be a plan, with timelines, to get process waste out of every part of the organization, which should be tied to the financials. Developing predictable processes will assist in becoming more accurate with the forecasts and eliminating waste that will provide true cost reductions, which Wall Street will be able to appreciate.

Operational Level of Leadership

The operational level of leadership includes director level employees and many managers. (In some smaller organizations, those at the Vice President level may have dual roles of strategic and operational responsibilities.) These responsibilities are clearly different than at the other two levels of the leadership continuum. Although there may be some involvement with 'in the trenches' employees at this level the critical responsibility is to ensure that they are operating in support and alignment with the strategic level. Leaders at this level are equally responsible for much of the planning, accountability, resources, communication, and ensuring that subordinates understand what needs to be achieved. This level often has direct level responsibility for some staff members. The operational leader focuses on how things will get done and the priority of what is to be done. Empowerment of subordinates and delegation are absolutely essential in this area.

Planning will include some scheduling activities, some need for balancing between functions, and a timeline of accountability to achieve the company's goals. Accountability should include metrics that they must manage as well as those metrics of the subordinate level. As an integrator, they must help translate the big picture into smaller chunks of 'how to's' between the other two levels. They must be close enough to the direct/operational level to help ensure process efficiency and that the barriers to customer expectations are overcome. Because they are close enough to the direct level and understand the strategic goals of the organization, they will have to help balance the resources needed to meet the objectives. This is critical because, although there needs to be some strategic involvement, they are expected to have some practical knowledge of the areas they are leading, and should know the process capabilities well enough to know the personnel needs or capital expenditure requirements to ensure the correct numbers of people and the right equipment is in place. Justifications for new capital expenditures should be led by this group, although the direct level should be intimately involved. Rarely should there be too many or not enough employees or wrong equipment, unless directed so by the strategic level of leadership. They must prepare information to support the needs of the organization and communicate to the strategic level. Although it may not be their responsibility to move forward with programs or projects, it is their responsibility to communicate needs to the strategic level and priorities to the direct level.

This level should help ensure that plant and/or supplier rationalization, low-cost countries initiatives, and all other programs and projects driven by the strategy have clear due diligence completed and communicated. The due diligence and recommendations for all programs and projects should be part of the strategy. This should be communicated to the strategic level of leadership to allow for better decisions and any updates needed for the organization. Periodic reviews of what is going on within the organization should be scheduled by this group to keep the strategic level informed and involved with what is going on. Although this might be the toughest chore for this level, as integrators they must try to get the strategic level leaders down on the shop floor as much as possible. If the strategic level of leadership is effective, they will be involved, frequently conducting skip level meetings and town halls with the employees. Walking around should also be second nature to operational leaders, ensuring that as they are working at training and developing the operational level, their process experiences are shared. At the operational level, there should be frequent opportunities for training and development of the direct level leaders, providing for succession planning and development that is essential at all levels of the continuum.

Direct/Tactical Level of leadership

At the direct or often called "tactical" level, this is where the rubber meets the road. At this level, throughout the organization, is where the expectations of the customer tend to be the most reflected. In a production environment, the quality of the product, cosmetics and functionality are the key focus. At this level, the leaders lead people and execute plans; they are involved in management. Much of the responsibility of the leaders at this level is to manage production schedules, metrics, lead the workers by example and train and develop the subordinates within the organization. It does not matter what the function, whether in operations, engineering, supply chain, or any of the support functions, direct level leadership helps illuminate the culture, and becomes a heartbeat of the organization. It is important that at this level of leadership that leaders understand the vision and strategy so they understand the impact and importance of what they provide. They must be linked through visibility to the other two levels, and this is where they become the purveyors of information upwards. It is critical for this level leader to understand the processes, people, and systems so that awareness can be provided to the operational level, as well as the strategic level. The operational level leaders should spend a great deal of time training and developing the leadership skills of this level, as well as to begin preparing them for the operational level. The strategic level should also spend time visiting this level, to help with training and development, and to ensure that the strategy is understood and being executed. The strategic level should also be receiving feedback at the same time and providing some guidance to the various processes. The direct level leader is perhaps the most challenging leadership role of the leadership continuum. They are faced all day/every day with the most complex task in the entire organization, and that is leading a group of individuals who are doing the actual work needed for the customer. They must deal with a variety of personalities, biases, likes, dislikes, levels of expertise, experience, reliability and strength of character and mold them into an efficient and effective team. The leaders at this level must be part psychologist, parent, enforcer, career counselor and be constantly in tune with the direction the organization is moving. Because many leaders leave college and start out at the operational and strategic levels of leadership, there is often a gross mis-calculation of the importance of this level. There needs to be a two-way sense of learning for those higher up the ladder that have not had the experience of working in this environment. It must be two-way to ensure the alignment of the leadership continuum is in place, and that the vision and strategy will be able to be understood and executed. The impact of this group on the current state of the business cannot be minimized. An eye should always be looking and as many ears as possible listening for ways to improve what is often the final stage of the business before a customer receives a product or service.

As we have looked at the roles and some of the responsibili-ties of leaders at the three different levels within an organization, it will be important to discuss another part. Just as we have provided a definition of a manager in the beginning of this section, it is impor-tant to not diminish this role. Organizations need managers to help execute their strategies. Everyone is not going to be a leader, and you need the role of manager to be able to execute directions provided by leaders. Managers are at or report to the tactical level leaders and manage specific tasks or areas of responsibilities and can be good tacticians. These are the people within organizations that have man-ager titles that are actually in leadership roles. Remember, all leaders have management skills; however, not all managers will be leaders.

Being in a leadership role does not make you a great leader. Part of the responsibility of a leader is to ensure that a business or company continues to become more efficient and more effective as you are reducing waste and cost from the organization. As we con-tinue to observe the vast number of companies in trouble, filing bankruptcies, and losing ground to the rest of the world, everyone must ask the question of why. How could the housing industry and mortgage crisis happen without earlier knowledge to Wall Street? How is the gas crisis happening? What about the dot com boom and bust? Why is the education system failing and who is responsible? Have the Big 3 automakers have become the "Next 3"? There are people leading and making a lot of money in all of these areas, but not performing their roles and responsibilities effectively. Is someone sleeping at the wheel or are we lacking people with the appropriate leadership skills leading many of our organizations? As many leaders are looking for Silver Bullets for their organizations to support the corporate pimps of Wall Street, they are struggling, trying to replicate what Toyota has done, what Harley Davidson has done, what Microsoft is doing, as well as some others, and not getting the magic results because there are no Silver Bullets! It will require great leadership, a clear vision, sound strategy, understanding the current state, effective processes, and a method of review (such as after action reviews) to replicate this kind of success.

LEADERSHIP AND PROCESS

As organizations become more aware of how inefficient they actually are, the more urgently many of those in leadership seek the Silver Bullets quick fixes to problems. They look for these when there is not an understanding of, or a true commitment to, solving the root causes of the problems. As we continue to move toward a global economy, we often end up compounding the problems exponentially by wanting more revenues, while not solving nor understanding the problems inherent with the current state of the business. Many people in leadership positions, and those on Wall Street, see and hear what they want, while not getting into the details enough to find out what is "really" going on.

The continued focus on outsourcing suppliers and manufacturing to low labor cost countries as a Silver Bullet to high labor costs ends up causing as many new problems as it hopes to solve. The major issue is that companies are attempting to grow their business and improve the bottom line by duplicate processes to build products or deliver services from overseas, when these same processes often do not function effectively or even exist domestically. How can you go to another country with different cultures and customs and hope that the business does better? There is also the issue of people. People that in some instances are ineffective and do not possess the competencies to be competitive domestically are also now leading these same organizations internationally. How can they change the paradigms in other countries?

The results we are seeing with respect to quality, safety, and similar added costs is causing many in leadership positions to reexamine their thoughts of whether the outsourcing ideas are actually as effective as once believed. It makes very little sense to export domestic leadership and process problems overseas, thinking that will make them magically go away, while expecting higher revenues through a reduced labor cost Silver Bullet. It is very interesting to note that as Toyota continues to build plants in the US, they are developing a high level of its suppliers within close proximity to these plants. While they are developing their processes in the US, many of the US companies are exporting their manufacturing businesses. I believe that if you have effective leadership and develop your business processes first before considering outsourcing, a shift in paradigms and leadership philosophy, like Toyota has developed, the savings in waste reduction you achieve may far outweigh some of the short-sighted low-cost labor initiatives now being sought after by many US companies.

Many organizations are attempting to duplicate what Toyota, Harley Davidson and a few other companies have been able to do. The difference is the short-term **want** without the long-term work that was involved in changing these organizations. It has taken Toyota over 50 years of change and learning to become one of the best automakers in the world. This is over 50 years of continuous improvement, learning, and the engagement of leaders throughout the leadership continuum working with employees and solving problems. Much of the key to their solving problems and creating solutions is having a clear understanding of what and where the sources of the problems are that cause the red ink on the balance sheet. The leadership team works with the employees to identify problems and provide solutions. They continuously work to have a clear picture of the current state of their operations, and they welcome issues and problems as opportunities to improve.

In the US, our automakers have not changed with the times; though in a few instances have just begun to listen to its employees who are close to where the problems are. There are other complications, with the union's refusal to change, pension plans, benefits costs, and other issues. Although very costly, there is still very little excuse for not providing good quality products that consumers actually want at a price they are willing to pay. In Lee Iacocca's book, "Where have all the Leaders Gone," he addresses many of these complicated issues, and expresses frustration with where we are headed as a country and economy.

It has taken Harley Davidson many years to return to prominence in the motorcycle industry, and even they are currently going through some significant organizational and business changes. Because of the economy and motorcycles sitting in dealers' showrooms, the motor company is being forced to look at costs and processes much closer that may have become bloated in the good times.

Many organizations are turning to "Silver Bullet" processes being supported by financial dreams pushed by boards, Wall Street, and many anxious managers trying to ensure their next bonus, but few are realizing long-term success. In an effort to duplicate what Toyota, Harley Davidson or few other companies have done to "change," these companies are creating un- or underfunded business operating systems, deploying lean and or six sigma programs, and anything else to impact the bottom without understanding that they must change and make a commitment. This change must be systemic as a culture or DNA of the company, and not reminiscent of a house of cards. Many of these programs are failing because of the quality of leadership and the lack of commitment.

I had a personal experience with one of my previous employers that wanted to create a Business Operating System. They wanted to create a system like Toyota, and began by hiring a very talented leader to start up the program. This senior leader had some successes utilizing Shingijitsu (an expert of the Toyota Production System, many of its senseis were a part of Toyota during the transformation) and some of the lean tools in his business unit.

He attempted to educate the leadership on what the journey would be, how we would attempt to move through the journey, and what it would require. With very little position power, resource support, or true active commitment from the senior leadership team, the level of success was almost predictable.

As we were trying to understand the current state of the organization, develop a business operating system (BOS), deploy training programs to support the development of competencies for master black belts, black belts, and green belts throughout the organization, we faced increased opposition from those in leadership positions that did not want to devote the time or resources. The sophistication of leadership and the understanding of the roles and responsibilities throughout the continuum was also a very large obstacle. We were clearly on a suicide mission: to grow the company, increase the efficiencies, and reduce cost, and this was to be done with the same quality of leadership and talent within the organization that had gotten it in the poorly run condition that it was in. Clearly a case of "if you always do what you always did, you will always get what you always got!" The more we began to uncover the current state the more resistance we received from the leadership team, who were more interested in collecting bonuses than solving problems. I am not suggesting that leaders should not get bonuses, because much of my financial rewards have come from being rewarded with these same bonuses. I am merely suggesting that there must be some sort of accountability and those bonuses should be based largely on performance. Many organizations (most that I have been a part of) have bonus programs that have a component of company and personal contributions. I am suggesting that the company and personal goals and objectives should be in alignment to ensure maximum bonus potential at all levels. If the company is doing well, then the bonuses should be paid to those that have contributed to that success, not to everyone just because they are there and are benefitting from the success. If the company is not doing well, then the bonus plan should be modified so that it is in alignment with the company's current state.

Having worked with some of the Shingijitsu teams in Japan and domestically, they had a similar sentiment, They did not believe that many of our companies would ever be successful deploying lean or using any of the other techniques they were teaching because of the poor quality of leadership. They indicated on many occasions that the focus on obtaining the belts and not always investing in the competencies of continuous improvement and lean would create obstacles to successes in many organizations. They were also very consistent with their thoughts on commitment and the engagement of leaders into the details of the businesses in the US. Getting involved with the people and processes closest to the shop floor and really understanding the inner workings of the businesses were also of great concern. In fact, there were many comments that the greatest fear of competition for the Japanese was the Koreans, not the Americans. Ironically, the quality of Korean cars has also become a great fear for the US economy and automakers. In a recent report from Consumer Reports, Honda, Toyota, and Subaru topped the list of best made cars. The quality of the Hyundai, Kia and others Korean-made cars has increased significantly.

Many companies today are looking at low-cost labor countries to move its products to save the bottom line, another case by leaders looking for a quick fix Silver Bullet to their financial concerns that are driven by Wall Street. We are experiencing quality problems, duplicating technology, safety issues, and many other issues while chasing the low-cost labor market. I am not suggesting that other people around the world are better or worse at running businesses than we here in the US, only that focusing on the relationship between leadership and process is paramount to the long-term commitment industry has to their customers and investors.

The art of leadership and the effectiveness of processes are critical to the success of any business. You must have a clear strategy that includes the level of details of the processes to ensure the desired financial outcomes are achieved. In later sections of this book, we will delve deeper into leadership, its roles and responsibilities, and processes.

Today, many organizations are seeking Silver Bullet solutions by trying to duplicate the Toyota Production System, or by implementing their own business operating system. Lean and six sigma program deployments are also being sought as Silver Bullets. It is not a surprise that many of these programs are not succeeding. They are not succeeding because the leadership in many instances does not understand its roles and responsibilities, does not have clearly aligned strategies, nor have a clear understanding of the commitment required to successfully deploy change. This too is not of great surprise when you look at how/where leaders are trained, and in many cases the pressure of outside influences such as bonus structures, Wall Street or even less involved boards.

As many companies try to define the pillars of a business operating system, or have training programs for lean, six sigma, master black belts, black belts and green belts without having an engaged leadership team that is clear in its strategy, successes will be difficult. The processes cannot replace the leadership and must be integrated and planned for in the strategy. A leader not involved in a company system, or who has a strategy that does not include process improvement, is as vulnerable as a strong process person that does not have the leadership skills to implement the programs. Some of the expertise acquired through the lean or six sigma training is great for projects, but other tools need to be involved to implement programs and systems.

Process skills are great for helping to improve processes, not running the entire business or being a Silver Bullet to impact change throughout the entire business. Leadership is needed. A good example of this is one of my personal experiences. As a martial artist with many years of training, with the focus being on a lifestyle of learning an art, I had the opportunity to compete with many that have actually gotten black belts in only a couple of years by learning the mechanics. Needless to say, those focused on paying for belts for personal gain never faired well in competition against those of us who took the time necessary to develop the competencies of the art.

This is similar to what is happening today in many companies. Many people are rushing to complete projects that may or may not be a priority in the business, with the focus of obtaining their "belts." The focus must be on competencies, and this should include a leadership component. The projects that people work on should be a part of a strategic plan that includes some sort of understanding of the value stream or current state of the entire business. The commitment to changing processes as a system should be planned to at least provide a payback to the organization, and be funded as such.

As the leadership looks strategically at its business, the voice of the customer, the quality of the product the customer expects, the rate they want it and the price they are willing to pay must be at the top of the list of items considered. All change should be planned and occur as a system company wide, not just in one or two parts of the organization, and must be driven from the top.

In a manufacturing company, change must be driven by leadership, and include sales, marketing, product/process engineering, supply chain, operations, customer service, and all of the transactional areas such as Human Resources (HR), Finance, IT, Legal, etc. This change must begin at the top, and a clear picture of the current state must be established. An understanding of the strengths, weaknesses, opportunities and threats of every area within the company must be explored. I am sure that this is a monumental task in many organizations, but this task in a failing business has the potential to provide real impact. We will explore this further as we look at strategy.

It is ironic that one of the key drivers in most process improvement initiatives is finance. They typically will want the results of these initiatives to provide bottom line, balance sheet results, but not support the resources needed for the change. Sometimes this change within the organization will require the status quo in HR, finance and all of the other support areas to change. This change is especially critical as we discuss leadership and process tools such as lean, six sigma, etc.

Human Resources

In Human Resources (HR), the change that is required to support a processed-based company will force a lot more attention to details within this segment of the organization. This attention to detail has to look at the strengths and weaknesses within the organization, its training programs, recruiting and retention policies, succession planning, and all of the internal programs that support the leadership of the company. Starting with the leadership team, HR must find ways to support the strengths of the organization starting with the C-level leadership. This means looking at the strategy and direction of the leadership and organization, focusing developmental needs, and recruiting on the weaknesses at this point of the organization. After looking at the senior leaderships, strengths, weaknesses and the direction of the organization, HR must begin to evaluate and help to ensure accountability within itself and all of the other functional areas of the company. It will be a futile attempt at success if you begin to implement a business operating system or lean policy deployment by starting in operations or any other singular function throughout the value stream without considering the whole of the system. The futility of this attempt is that the entire business, value stream, or system is interconnected and dependent on each other for overall success. As HR is working with the senior leadership team, it must look at its own processes in regards to compensation, benefits, evaluations, succession planning and the other corporate governance policies, as well as the functions it performs. They must begin, along with the leadership, to ensure that consistency is in place and that it is supporting the process-driven environment. After all, you will be looking to a workforce that is engaged, supporting the needs of the business, and being rewarded for ensuring the success of the business. As many organizations look at change, it is imperative that the leadership team incorporate all of the required changes to the system or value stream as part of the strategic plan of the organization. It also must be communicated, supported and followed throughout. For HR, the accountability to be a partner and fully engaged in the change is critical. HR should have clear metrics that are fully aligned with the strategy and needs of the organization. HR should also be involved in every aspect of the business in some form to help ensure that its part of the partnership and change initiatives are successful.

Finance

For an organization to change to a lean environment, the system by which costs are calculated becomes much different. Savings should actually become predictable, based on the processes, and the financials should become the result of the predictable processes and needs of the customers. The focus change incorporates a dependency on the accuracy of a system based on the customer. This will be a seminal change in some organizations; it may also be a huge challenge for Wall Street to digest. However, as many organizations are discussing implementing some of the process tools, they must also look at the long-term benefits change in the Finance department.

We need to lose old paradigms! We need to think in terms of processes, not transactions. We need to think Cost Management, not Cost Accounting. We need to be leading teams, not reporting history. We are not going to go in after the war, count the dead bodies, and report the results to top management. Finance and Accounting should be proactive, and must get into the trenches with the troops. We need to eliminate the myopic behavior created by Standard Cost, and the game playing associated with Absorption Accounting.

Traditional financial accounting utilizes Standard Cost and Absorption Costing. These cost systems were useful back in 1930, but not today. Standard Cost is last year's most representative actual, and is not going to drive any business to new heights of profitability. It is also a complex system that is not designed to give us information in a timely fashion nor in a useful format for continuous improvement. It gives us data, not information for decision-making. Standard Cost is inventory driven, but in lean we have no inventory as we "make to order." Standard Cost may be suitable for financial accounting, but it does not help us manage the business.

Absorption Cost was useful when businesses were producing products in mass. That is not the case today. Today we need a new management accounting system that aligns with lean manufacturing operations; an accounting system that focuses on Value Streams and processes, not on departments and functional silos. We need a system that also focuses on speed of delivery to the customer and continuous improvement. Some believe that Activity Based Cost is the answer. Activity Based Cost, like Standard Cost, is too complex and requires an army of people and elaborate computer systems to operate. Activity Based Cost only reallocates cost. It does not help us eradicate cost. Activity Based Cost focuses on activities, not resources.

The answer to today's quest for a management cost system that supports lean is a combination of Target Cost and Actual Cost; a system that shows the true results of our lean implementation efforts, focuses on the customer and our Value Streams. Our traditional financial statements do not show our lean results because the fruits of our work in lean are not all recorded in the G/L (General Ledger). Lean Accounting will give us better decision-making data presented in a language understandable to all employees in the business, and in a format upon which we can act. The goal of lean is to improve profits while pleasing our customer. Lean Accounting will help us reach that goal!

Finance must be involved in the business units to ensure that the support needed from a financial perspective within the processes is evident. They should be close enough to each aspect of the business to help ensure alignment of metrics and deliverables to the customer are met. Finance should also have their metrics aligned with the strategy, and help to ensure support that metrics throughout the organization are consistent and aligned.

As we look at improving the bottom lines of organizations, and appeasing the corporate pimps from Wall Street, change has to occur with top leadership ensuring that the strategy and accountability of the entire value stream is changing simultaneously, and not individually. The above examples of Human Resources and Finance are just the tip of the iceberg of requirements needed for change to actually and effectively occur. Those companies that are only focusing on a few continuous improvement methods and tools within operations, supply chain or other portions can attest to the lack of progress based on their own experiences. We will look at all of the areas as a system when we get into the strategic portion of this book.

Leadership must provide the playbook, which includes how things are going to be accomplished, and they must know how the processes or activities are going to be done so that they know how the accomplishments or scores are kept while they are occurring. The review of these successes and failures will help adjust the way things are going and, if needed, to rethink some of the strategic objectives.

I have had the opportunity to visit many plants and companies around the world that are running kaizens or have some lean tools in place, and to see the joy on the leaders' faces is amazing. The concern is that when you ask some of the employees the overall goal or plan, they often do not know. They do not know how the processes are interrelated or how they impact the larger picture. At the direct or tactical levels of leadership, the success is exciting but if it is not aligned with the operational or strategic levels of leadership, it will never gain the traction or the true savings required to sustain momentum. This is another example of leadership and process not being in alignment and a strategy that is not effective.

Many companies ask Shingijitsu to come to their organizations to run week-long kaizens with the employees and the experienced senseis. This is typically a very expensive engagement that is focused on a particular area of the plant where there are obvious flow, waste or production problems. The areas receiving attention are typically fixed for that week, the employees are happy and a big paycheck cut to Shingijitsu. Unless these engagements are continuous or tied to a value stream or some other strategy, the success is usually short lived. It is short lived because the processes must be linked to the systems upstream and downstream of the problems. This is also a Silver Bullet attempt of training the trainer to fail. A leadership problem!

The proper manner to which leadership meets process here, is that as part of the strategy or after a value stream map has been created, the impact and priorities of the projects or kaizens should be planned. This planning should allow everyone to understand the order, priority, and outputs of the event. As the team reviews the big picture impact, the interdependencies of the kaizen are also addressed. If you are working on a kaizen in a particular cell, and you are overproducing (one of the eight wastes), the supply chain will be able to do its part in the change, as will human resources. If a reallocation of people is needed, finance will provide justification from a cost perspective, engineering from a design or work instructions perspective, and so on. It is a required system change on almost every kaizen or project. The system, just like a well-oiled machine or human body, must move as one. This is a process issue that requires leadership to ensure that all parts of the machine are moving simultaneously, and should be a part of the strategy that includes continuous or process improvement. This is how true savings begin, and not through finance manipulating numbers from an office far from any of the operational areas.

The importance of leadership and process is of paramount importance, and they must be in alignment to be effective. Leadership must plan for a certain amount of process improvements with the appropriate resources as part of its strategy, and with these processes being defined; finance becomes more accurate in reporting the expectations to the leadership, shareholders or employees.

As many businesses continue to focus on the number of kaizens that are done (master black belts, black belts, and green belts that are going to be developed in the organizations), without considering how and where or even if the continuous improvement activities are being included in the strategy, failure will continue. Many organizations are continuing to use these tools as window dressing, and some are just dropping the programs, saying that they are too expensive, they do not have time, or they are not realizing the results they had expected. This is clearly a leadership problem, where the leadership was hoping the process improvements would be the Silver Bullet that creates miracles while they never take the time to develop a cohesive plan.

Most organizations, plants and businesses are in existence based on a payback period and plan to make a profit. This period normally has a formula. For example, in manufacturing it is often common for capital equipment and justifications for other high-dollar expenditures to focus on a payback and a certain expectation of efficiency. In the US, an 85% Overall Equipment Effectiveness (OEE) is what we typically use for our organizations, and we try to look at a 2 year payback on most equipment. With many organizations hovering around 20 to 30% effectiveness, the business will normally be losing money from day 1, payback will not be realized as planned, and problems will persist. As you can tell in an organization running between 20 to 30% efficiency, it is hardly a waste of time to focus on improvement. While many of our financial plans are based on an 85% OEE, I do not recall being in a plant in the US that was close to operating at this rate. Having visited numerous plants around the world, only in Japan, was the rate even close to being met, because their expectations were different than ours. It may only be a matter of semantics, but in my opinion Continuous Improvement starts at the rate of expected effectiveness you calculated when you purchased the business or equipment, not at the rate you are losing money. Continuous improvement is not a system to lower the rate of losses, although most of the tools it uses can certainly help turn a situation around. From a morale perspective, the unvarnished truth of the current state of the business should almost always be communicated as such and should be included in the strategy or plan! It is also part of the process that should help in understanding the entire Voice of Customer concept it is centered on (when the customer expects the product, what they are willing to pay, and at what level of quality they expect delivery).

Leadership is an art, that has a lot of responsibility, and the processes should be made so that the repeatability and reliability will help them understand the needs of the customer, and the company's ability to meet these needs better than the competition.

So as companies continue to invest millions of dollars in creating business operating systems, developing lean and six sigma programs, they should focus first on the leadership. This focus must include a look at a complete strategy that answers the how to's of execution and not the financials, which are normally less than accurate, and definitely not as predictable as they would be in lean accounting. This investment is a huge undertaking if the organization is committed, and must include every function in the system or value stream. This includes, in a manufacturing company, senior leadership, sales, marketing, engineering, supply chain, operations, customer service, and the transactional areas, including HR, finance, IT, and legal. It will be very difficult, if not impossible, to focus on just one or two areas of the company, such as operations, supply chain, or engineering, without the others, as many companies are doing today. Leadership must be intimately involved with how the processes of the company are doing, so that they will be more efficient focusing on the strategy, strengths and weaknesses of the organization and the competition. It will be very difficult to beat the competition, regardless of market conditions, if you as a leader are not clear as to what's going on in your own organization. It will also be very difficult to convey to the analysts of Wall Street or investors of a business what you will deliver as a profit when the condition or predictability of your processes within your company is a mystery. Yes, there are some other mitigating circumstances that have impact on many companies, such as gas prices, steel prices, and other commodities. These will cause change, but understanding where your process capabilities are can surely help with other decisions, other than implementing layoffs or immediate pricing changes.

During my time in the homebuilding industry, it was very shocking to learn that many of the homebuilders did not know how much it cost to build a home. They did know how much they paid, because of the invoices. But managements understanding of where the actual value of what they had been paid for in building a home was a mystery to them. In one of my operations we tried to run time studies on the work being completed on the homes, but were quickly deterred because the subcontractors did not want us to understand what they were doing and the times actually involved. The relationship between many in leadership roles and the subcontractors ensured that the root cause of cost remained a mystery. Ironically, the new system of building homes we were creating, where the cost structure could be clearly defined, was being compared to the traditional construction methods, to which no one knew what the costs were. It was even more shocking to know that many of the subcontractors did not know how much their process were costing or how the estimating was being done. In some instances, this was because of variation in land conditions or other issues, but this seemed to be the norm for the industry. In two different companies the subcontractors' submitted invoices, a multiplier was added, and the total was charged to the homebuyer. As you can imagine, the profits in building a home are great! This lack of process knowledge is definitely a leadership issue. However, because of the delta in profits and individual salaries at the leadership levels, the only ones impacted were the buyers. The aerospace industry experienced a similar nightmare, and again the impact of lack of process knowledge would typically be passed on to the US government, municipalities or other entities that were buying the product. Ultimately, this lack of leadership process understanding will impact the everyday citizen of the US. I am not advocating that companies should not make a profit, but clearly understanding what products and services cost and developing processes that are repeatable and reliable will be a huge gain to every company. Many of us have heard of the $75 hammer being sold to the US government, and you must ask how much does it actually cost? How does this happen? And who pays for it? It is a leadership and process issue!

As we begin to look at the section in this book called Strategies, we will take a deeper look into some examples of the level of detail the different areas of the system or value stream will need to explore if the change to a more successful environment is to occur.

The Organizational Journey

<u>If you don't know where you are going</u>
<u>you might wind up someplace else.</u>
Yogi Berra

As we begin to explore one of the most important tasks of the strategic leader, we will focus on the criticality of this function. In this section we will explore the "where and how" journey of an organization most commonly referred to as the vision and strategy. If the person in a leadership role gets this part of leading right, they will experience a good sense of satisfaction. If they do not get this right, failure for the leader and crisis and chaos for the organization will occur. The leader, through experience and training, should have an idea individually as to where they might want to take the organization. This should occur as one of the first tasks of this position when a new person takes the reins. This is commonly called "Envision" (To have mental imagine in advance of realization; to picture to one self; to look forward.) This does not necessarily have to occur after a significant amount of data has been gathered, and may be less accurate than definitive, but it provides an idea of where the organization might be able to go. This can be a lonely task, relies primarily on judgment, and is more purely hypothetical than scientific. The reason for this comment is because the leader must be able to see the potential of the organization, outside of what might have become status quo. The leader will have to envision the organization in an end state and understand its full potential, and then couple it with the data, knowledge, and expertise of their staff and the whole organization to begin building the vision statement. Being a leader is often a lonely job, and as the picture of organizational effectiveness comes into focus, the leader must begin to assess the strengths and weaknesses of the staff and organization; they cannot take anything for granted. A leader without individually conceived concepts or thoughts of where to take an organization cannot be called a leader. After all, a new leader is typically being brought in because something has changed or needs to change. I am focusing on the new leader because establishing a vision and mission should be one of the primary functions of this person. And if there are no fresh new ideas, the company is in trouble from day one.

VISION/MISSION

Where are we going?

Whether you are starting a new business, taking over the reins of an existing one or implementing changes within your current organization, establishing the vision/mission is one of the most important tasks that every leader must provide. The vision is a simple statement of WHERE the leader intends to take the organization. The mission is WHAT you are going to do to achieve this.

> **Vision***: a vivid concept, or object of imaginative contemplation; a mode or way of seeing, discernment or foresight; to manifest to sight (to make something to be seen). A vision normally has no foundation, as in a scheme or project,*
> **Mission:** *a specific task given to a person or group, the chief function or responsibility of an organization or institution, that which one is destined or fitted to do,*

The word vision is straightforward in its definition, but is often confused with something more complex. A vision statement can often be found on plaques on walls around companies, on business cards, and often may be communicated to Wall Street, and throughout the organization. Many companies have them, though there are some that do not. Vision is the first step in taking the organization anywhere!

The mission is not a matter of hope; it is not a vision or process, it is the essential direction you are headed! Senior leaders must be able to articulate an organizational direction and the vision/mission is the starting point for molding the direction of the organization. A vision that is understood, communicated and utilized throughout the organization provides the strategic, operational, and direct leaders with one of the primary tools they need to take an idea and see it through to completion. There must be a vision of an end state, and where the organization is going, for the team to know that the ideas they are acting on compliment and build towards that end state. It will often be a good idea to involve the senior staff and other key individuals around the organization in establishing the mission because the leader must begin to know the marketplace, the customers, what players they have on the team, the current state of the organization, and what success should look like as quickly as possible. The senior leader should have gotten some information on the current state of the business and personally envisioned where it can go, through their hiring process, so this can be done as the senior leader comes on board and some initial assessments have been completed. This may take a few weeks to a few months depending on the size of the organization. A senior leader has the right to drive the organization where they see fit, but it is very helpful to have some data about the organization, and ensure that needed support is garnered during this phase, and that the organization has or can obtain the resources needed to realize the goal.

Your vision conveys the message 'Why we are in business,' but it is the mission that gives your vision teeth and tells everyone what you are going to do about it. The Mission statement is the beginning of where the rubber meets the road in the strategic planning process. Charting a course that is not viable for the organization because of conditions, finances, talent, market position, or processes could be a costly decision that will undermine the credibility of the vision.

Vision and mission development have been expounded on at length in many venues, but it is the next step in the process, building a solid strategic plan that will ultimately decide if your venture will succeed or fail. Too many organizations seem to think that having a great vision and mission statement is the 'be all, end all,' and selling that with the proper PR support is the road to riches. Whereas, if your goal is to develop a strong business that can survive the test of time you are going to need to know HOW you are going to get where you want to go. You need to build a strategy.

STRATEGY

Strategy: *the science and art of employing strength to secure the objective; planning; maneuver; a careful plan or method or a clever scheme for gaining an end; a cunning plan to gain an end.*

Strategy, Vision and Mission are clearly different in their definitions, but more importantly in the purpose that they provide to an organization or business. The vision and mission provides the 'where' the organization is going, and the strategy provides the 'how to' or execution plan to arrive at the end state. They are closely aligned, and one without the others will establish an environment of failure for a leader and the organization. Some of the best examples of setting a vision without the right conditions is evident in many companies but best understood in athletic teams. Take, for example, all 32 teams in the NFL, all teams in the NBA, and the MLB begin their seasons with a clear vision or end state. They are all looking to win the championship of their respective sports. As you and I know, there will ALWAYS be only one champion, and the rest will be considered losers! This is because certain conditions needed to support the vision have become obstacles. This could be a matter of leadership, talent, competition, finances, skills, or processes that can each have a huge impact on why teams are not successful. It is not much different in the business world, the failure to have a good strategy or to properly execute that strategy is clearly a reason why some teams never win the championship, and some companies fail or never reach their full potential.

The strategy or strategic planning portion of a senior leader's role is very complex and time consuming, but again it is one of the key functions of this position. It is very complex because planning how an organization will achieve its goals will require a great deal of assessments and understanding of the current state so as to formulate the best path to achieve the desired end state. This must include an analysis of the people, processes and systems of the organization. What is working well, what is not, and a plan to address all that are not. It is also important to understand why some things are working well so that you can ensure that things are not working by luck or hope. You must understand or have a good way of assessing the marketplace and your competition. As you look at the current state, which we will discuss a little later, the leader must understand where the opportunities are in the organization. As the business or market changes, you must know where you have flexibility. Who is on the team, how effective are they, and how are things measured? How are things communicated through the organization? How are decisions made? Do you have a good accountability system in the organization and are they aligned through every function? How does your organization flow, and where are the bottlenecks and waste?

A good tool to assess the current state is called a Value Stream Map (VSM), which can help to map out the entire organization, allowing you to see a map of the entire organization or by functional processes. This is another tool that works in concert with a 3-year strategy matrix. We will discuss the 3-year strategy matrix tool later in this section.

1.   What does the customer want? When do they want it? What price are they willing to pay for it?
2.   How things flow from one function to another.
3.   It will also highlight how long it takes for a product or service to move through a particular function.
4.   Bottlenecks and waste can be calculated and highlighted.
5.   What equipment do you have? How is it being maintained? Do you have enough or too much?
6.   How are your facilities and office space laid out?
7.   Do you have enough people in the organization, or to many?
8.   Do you have a business operating system in your organization, and how effective is it?
9.   What about your programs and projects? Which ones are successful, and why? Why are they not successful?
10. How effective are your processes throughout the organization, through every function?
11. How are the processes measured?
12. How often do your leaders visit the front lines?
13. Does finance drive your organization, or does processes?

14. Do you have heroes and goats every month, and quarter, being driven by the financial system manipulations that are occurring? Moving product or services during this time to meet Wall Street commitments?

15. Are you manipulating the sales or production numbers to fit the need?

16. What about your suppliers? What is the quality of product that is coming in from them? How much is it costing, and when is it being delivered? Are there opportunities to help your suppliers to become more efficient, or do you treat them as an outsider of your organization, similar to what the failing auto industry does?

17. How are you defining and calculating investing in low labor cost countries to get products or services? What does your organization know about the culture, customs or conditions of these areas? Do you have people within your company versed in these areas and, most importantly, able to train talent in a different culture? A good clue here is that if things are not working well domestically in your organization, going over to low-cost countries where there are even more complexities to deal with will not work well. How will safety, logistics cost, quality, or timeliness be impacted by the low-cost countries. (Without naming an organization, one task in a role that I held previously, the CEO gave an edict that approximately 30% of the supplied parts should be from low-cost countries. There was going to be a significant savings to the organization with this move. An organization that was under-resourced and light on talent moved forward as the edict was given, without a strategy or a clear vision, I am sure you can imagine the results of this action.)

18. How strong is the relationship with your customers and what are their expectations?

19. Is sales or engineering leading new product development? Is this being driven by the customer?

20. How are you receiving the voice of the customer? Gut feel or data?

These are just a few of the questions involved in creating a thorough plan or strategy. Throughout this book, I use the term "holistic strategy" to define a strategic plan. Because there are so many organizations that use 'financial plans' as their strategy, I did not want there to be any mistake as to the intent here. A holistic strategy is more definitive and encompasses every function within an organization. Whereas, the financial plan, which I have seen numerous times, is driven by financial numbers that often cannot be supported by unpredictable or inefficient processes. As indicated, the financials should be the predictable result of effective processes and driven by them, not the other way around. There will be times that the two may not be in alignment; however, this should be the exception not the norm. There are other key functions that must be completed by the finance team, but most of their production data should be predictable, not assumed. Unless the finance team is close to every function within the business system it will be very hard for them to accurately define the number of deliveries, timing and costs. Even if they are close to the functions, inefficient processes will still result in poor financial predictability. Remember, inefficiencies throughout the organization will impact all of these numbers.

Every leader MUST have a strategy. It should be simple, succinct and understood by everyone in the organization. The level of details will change as responsibilities move down through the leadership continuum; however, the communication and alignment must be advanced back up to senior leadership. You should never abandon the strategy if things get tough, or assets are not being brought to bear to their greatest advantage; this is when you adapt and forge ahead.

There are three key areas to focus on for a strategy: External Analysis, Internal Analysis and Analysis of Alternatives. Without all of these areas being addressed and analyzed a plan cannot be considered a holistic strategy, and the organization will not reach its full potential and some instances will fail. The three key areas are:

1. External Analysis
    i.   The customer
         a.   How strong is the relationship with your customers?
         b.   What are their expectations?

        c.   How are you receiving the voice of the customer?
        d.   What complaints and criticisms do they have?
        e.   Clarity in understanding the needs of internal customers with the same expectations as external customers for products or services.

  ii.   The competition

        a.   Who is it?
        b.   What are their strengths?
        c.   What are their weaknesses?
        d.   How are you dealing with them?

2. Internal Analysis

  i.   People

        a.   Assessment plan.
        b.   Succession planning.
        c.   Training and development, not just HR-driven but by all leaders.
        d.   Recruiting process, tied to vision and strategy.
        e.   Retention plans should be maintained for those that fit within the vision and strategy, as well as have the competencies needed for the organization. Those that do not should be given the opportunity to get these skills, and if they do not, should be moved out of the organization.
        f.   Evaluation processes.
        g.   Compensation program tied to performance.

  ii.   Process

        a.   Define business operating system for the company.
        b.   Assessment process to determine the current state of processes.
        c.   Communication methods and frequency (including vision, mission, strategy, town halls, and state of business meetings for all employees).
        d.   Change implementation and continuous improvement programs such as lean, six sigma and ISO must be included in the strategy so they are properly resourced; otherwise, they will not be integrated in the DNA and culture

      e.   Accountability plans for every function.

      f.   Plan for common metrics, companywide. Every process of every function should be measured and focused on three primary areas to meet the customers' expectations (1, timely delivery; 2, cost the customer is willing to pay; and 3, quality or fit and form they expect).

      g   The methods of reporting throughout the leadership continuum should be aligned and cascaded across the organization.

      h.   Delegation and empowerment should be defined in the strategy.

      i.   After Action Review process (for learning organization).

  iii. Systems

      a.   What information systems will be used in the company? Oracle, SAP, etc.

      b.   What business operating system will be used and implemented?

      c.   Communication methods for the company. Toyota uses a status code for every function within company, and with focus on this system, can identify bottlenecks and deal with issues immediately.

      d.   Must have an assessment process.

3. Analysis of alternatives

      a.   SWOT analysis.

      b.   Rationalization programs for internal operations and suppliers.

      c.   Expanding business or operations to other countries or regions.

      d.   Exploring low-cost countries.

      e.   New programs or new ways of dealing with business.

      f.   Continuous improvement programs.

      g.   Employee programs.

      h.   Customer-based programs, etc.

    i.   Product development.
    j.   New systems.
    k.   Expansion.
    l.   Culture change.

Although I indicate that a strategy should be kept simple, "Simple" in this context means that the strategic statement must be succinct and easily understood. If a leader cannot explain, in general terms, the strategy in about 25 words, it may be too complex or, even worse, not clear to the leader who is attempting to communicate it. You will notice that in each of the above areas that I included having an assessment process. A leader must understand the current state of a business, a business unit or an individual function before just plowing ahead and attempting changes. The above outline represents a highlight of the things that need to be included in the strategic planning processes. Please note that a Strengths, Weaknesses, Opportunities and Threats, most commonly referred to as SWOT, analysis is included as one of the tools in the Analysis of Alternatives section. This is one of the most commonly used and most familiar tools people will mention when developing a strategy. There are many people that believe this will lead to a strategy; however, it is only one piece of the process. It is a high-level view of an organization and its competition, but it does not delve into the level of detail or completeness required within a holistic or complete strategy. It is evident that the development and execution of any strategy involves a complex process, and this process stays the same whether it is being executed by the CEO of a Fortune 500 company or the owner of a small business. The process needs to be the same, but the level of complexity of the issues will be different. Depending on the size of the organization, there will be things that are needed to be added to the list; in some instances the verbiage may change. As a leader begins to develop the strategy, in an organization, the more complete their understanding of the current state the better the plan will be. The current state of the organization and understanding, what your true capabilities are, instead of hoping, will allow you to be realistic about growing your business and satisfying your customer's requirements.

When you look at the time required, or the complexities involved in setting a strategy, you can see why many organizations take a different path. If you look at the Iraq War, the president might have had a vision, but the strategy was definitely not complete. The result of this can be seen when looking at the current state of the Iraq war, which is seen by many as a disaster with no clearly defined end state.

Without becoming embroiled with the current political situation but looking at the major issues that are topics of communication for all candidates in the 2008 Presidential primaries, the candidates are discussing the war, the economy, healthcare, and the education system to mention a few. Without taking any sides to this issue, you can see a direct correlation with our discussion of building a business. Let's take the current healthcare system for example. Most everyone agrees that it would be great for everyone to have effective, affordable healthcare. There are a few "current state" issues that might need to be addressed.

1. How will this be paid for?
2. Why are the costs of healthcare rising?
3. What about the litigation lotto?
4. The education system that produces our doctors and nurses is not efficient.
5. The shortage of healthcare professionals.
6. The emergency rooms are overloaded and understaffed.

Hospitals are backlogged; there are poor processes throughout many of their operational and support functions. With the shortages of personnel and a fear of lawsuits facing many in the healthcare industry, many hospitals are not as effective today as they could be and many healthcare employees are overworked. How will they handle an influx of millions of other Americans into the hospital system that would come as a result of some of the proposals put forth by the various campaigns? I recently saw on Good Morning America where there are businesses starting up that are sending in "spy patients" to evaluate how doctors are performing, as well as the overall experience at hospitals and medical centers across the US, which we know are severely broken. As you can imagine, the doctors and hospital administrators are not taking to this kindly. This is almost like throwing gasoline on a fire that has been burning for years. I am not sure that sending undercover patients in to evaluate a system that is known to be broken and take up the time of already overworked healthcare workers is the right answer. We must get to the root cause of these issues and develop better leadership, holistic strategies, an understanding the current state of the healthcare system, tighter accountability, and some regulations on the litigation lotto to impact the cost of healthcare. There must also be an extension of accountability to the insurance companies that are in a race with the oil and gas companies to see who can make the most money while helping the fewest number of people.

Although the presidential candidates might have a strategy to support their vision or campaign slogans, I am sure an in-depth look at the current state would force the focus on many other areas. Why is there a shortage of personnel? What about the turnover rates? How long does it take to train these individuals? Do we have some sort of standardization or quality checks of the personnel coming out of the many universities or colleges? After all, out of a graduating class of 500 doctors, you will not know whether your doctor was number 1 or 499. How are the individuals trained once they have completed the formal education process, and how long does this take? Who is addressing the processes within the hospital system? What is the true quality of the healthcare you receive? What about the influence the pharmaceutical companies have on the healthcare industry? How about technology, and how it is being shared with other hospitals? Some hospitals are using laparoscopic methods for a variety of procedures while many are still using traditional methods of surgery. Who is regulating the requirement for training and how will this impact an influx of millions of other Americans. The feedback I have gotten from sources in the medical profession is that some doctors will not go back through the training. It is often not cost effective for them to go through additional training when their pay is not increasing. What about the impact of proposed changes on the quality of the education system that must produce these healthcare workers? It is great fodder for candidates to look at these types of issues and propose broad encompassing programs; however, I hope there are a greater number of people looking at how these programs will be implemented and if they can be successful. If not, they will end up just as W's war in Iraq or Ford Motor Company's SUV strategy (or the auto industries failure to provide hybrid or energy efficient vehicles). A good look at the current state will be critical to the success of any business, hospital or government. Accountability of how well these programs have performed, through "After Action Review" programs (which we will discuss later in the book), might help the success rate or, at a minimum, learning what to do differently for the next program.

I had the opportunity to build a Greenfield organization (from the ground up) during my tenure as President of a manufacturing division for Pulte Homes. During this time my staff and I created a vision and a very thorough strategy. Because our current state was not very complex, the process was very straightforward. We went offsite to build our vision, mission and strategy. We looked at where we wanted to take the organization, and how we would get there. We looked at every aspect of the business, people, process and systems. We looked at our customers and competition as we began to enter our new product into the market place. Every function in the organization participated, and we ensured alignment of all of the employees in the organization. Although we had a good process, there was not an effective strategy for our support from the corporation or the operating division that we worked with. Because of the lack of a clear vision or strategy within the corporation, although it was the founder's program, the program failed. It failed because the cost to produce the homes in a down market had not been anticipated, and what appeared to be some ethical issues with the subcontractors this program would have replaced.

The importance of creating a strategy in today's markets cannot be taken lightly. There is also a need to constantly evaluate the strategy as the market and the current state change. It is important to understand the current state of the business, which we will look at in the next part of this book.

CURRENT STATE OF THE BUSINESS

We have reviewed the roles and responsibilities of leaders at different levels and what their roles might be. We have also reviewed the importance of the strategic planning process as an all encompassing holistic strategy. We will now begin to look at another critical part of being a leader. It is the understanding and accepting of the current state of the business. This is sometimes very tough because you have to kick over a lot of trees and rocks to understand what is actually going on in the business and the business units, instead of just listening to the staff. And, the leader must be able to make this unbiased assessment while maintaining a clear view of what he has envisioned for the organization. It is true that you have to trust your staff in many instances; however, as indicated in the leadership portion of this book, this is part of the importance of understanding the strengths and weaknesses of your staff (what they know vs. what they do not, so you know what to teach). It is also important to lead by walking around and actually seeing the business, talking with employees at almost every level, and having meaningful metrics for every part of your business. By coupling the walk around concept with a well communicated policy that encourages an open environment where people are free to communicate concerns without fear of retribution for things that are not going well, you will be better able to develop an accurate current state assessment. Accountability of everyone within the organization and or business units to the strategy will be critical to the success of the endeavor. Knowing the current state of the business is necessary so that not only will you have a clear indicator of where your business is, and what is going on, but you will also be able to stay on track with your strategy.

I have had a number of experiences throughout my career where a strategy (actually a financial plan) was thought to be created, but a clear understanding of the current state of the business and business units were never assessed. A good example was during my time at Harley Davidson, where we were working on a long-term plan and manufacturing was gearing up for increased capacity to satisfy growing demand. This was a great time of prosperity for many at

Harley Davidson because there was a huge backlog and many people were waiting 12 to 18 months to get their much-wanted Harleys. The stocks were doing extremely well, and throughout the organization (including the shop floor) many were becoming wealthy. The customers would often have to pay the dealers to get on a waiting list to get their bikes and often they would not even get to choose the color of bike they wanted, but would be satisfied with the chance to be a rebel and owner of the new American dream. Wall Street was very happy.

As the company focused with great diligence on supporting customer demands, engineering, manufacturing, supply chain, and the aftermarket teams focused primarily on getting more and more volume and hence revenue generation. The company spent a great deal of money on new product development, new processes and ideas for bikes, capital equipment, hiring employees, new facilities, supplier development programs, and a host of other activities. There were some conscious efforts made to continue the Close to the Customer concept, by gaining greater visibility with the Harley Owners Group programs as well. The Harley Owners Group or HOG was an important catalyst to the customer feedback and engagement process for the motor company. The Close to the Customer concept and getting direct customer feedback was one of the major pillars of Harley Davidson's success.

Wall Street, the employees, many customers and investors were extremely happy with the prosperity and financial success that Harley Davidson was bringing. It was a great run from the early 80s, after the 13 executives from Harley Davidson bought the company from AMF, until shortly after the 100th anniversary in 2003.

Rich Teerlink and Jeff Bleustein, the former CEOs of Harley Davidson, were great leaders during the turnaround. As many organizations have fun during the good times, many often do not discuss the bad times and problems that occurred during the times of prosperity. As we were growing, we focused a great deal in moving forward (revenues), but I believe that there could have been more time spent developing a holistic strategy and understanding the current state of the business across the organization. In manufacturing, there was a tremendous amount of effort focused on growth. However, very few people were focused on the waste being built into the processes. There were many people within the organization certified in lean, through the University of Kentucky and other programs, but very few people were being held accountable for reducing waste throughout the organization. I led the development for some of the first lean tools within a couple of areas at Harley Davidson, and there were a couple of people that focused on trying to understand cost and reducing waste, but not many. Because of the prosperity that was being experienced, there was more focus on production, less focus on cost or waste, and a lot of leniency for expenses and having fun throughout the organization. There was no accountability standard applied consistently across manufacturing, supply chain, or engineering. Although there was some good leadership, the development of a clear picture of the current state would have yielded the opportunity for some additional work in the areas of people, processes and systems. A process focus would have highlighted some of the waste within the manufacturing, engineering and supply chain that would have allowed the organization to be prepared for times not of the same prosperity that the growth years produced. While there was a huge focus on the relationship between the salaried and hourly employees across the organization, there were clearly some areas that performed at levels below expectations that required additional resources to keep up with the pace of growth. The added labor component in certain areas was a clear sign that we were not achieving the 85% OEE that had been built into the financial plans. OEE is defined as Productivity x Availability x Yield. This calculation is often used to determine the payback for a piece of capital equipment or often a facility; 85% is often used as it shows a reduction in available people hours due to lunch and breaks during a normal work shift. We used this standard frequently at Harley Davidson to help with capital purchases and financial planning. There were a number of capital expenditures that we were purchasing with an expected 2-year payback. In many cases, we prepared the necessary payback to ensure that the calculations met the 2-year requirement, but we did not address the operational issues to ensure we met the efficiency rates needed for this payback scenario. Without understanding the current state of efficiencies or with a plan to eliminate waste, Harley

Davidson as well as many other organizations would never meet the planned paybacks for equipment and facilities. Rarely would we go back and review how effective our estimates or predictions were after the equipment had been purchased. In various venues, I have utilized the After Action Review (AAR) to learn from the purchasing process in an effort to become more accurate in developing capital expenditures. A current state process review would have been very helpful, if it were aligned with the strategic planning processes, providing for greater predictability within the changing markets.

In an environment where the backlog was in many cases almost 2 years, the expectations and accountability for the sales force produced a different focus. As manufacturing, engineering, supply chain, and aftermarket was focused on ramping up during the 80s and 90s, a current state of the sales team would have revealed some great opportunities with people, processes and systems, and most importantly new markets. As an organization, we knew we needed to look at appealing to younger riders and developing more customer diversity with women and minorities. I personally paid for and sponsored a study to highlight what many minorities were riding, why they were riding other brands, and why they were not riding Harley Davidson's. I focused on key areas across the country that had high concentrations of minorities riding bikes. The focus was on New York, New Jersey, Philadelphia, Texas, Florida, and California. I did this because as an organization we knew that the riders were increasing in age and there was a need to attract new riders. I knew for a fact there had been an increase in ridership amongst African Americans, Latinos and other minorities. The results were very clear. Minority ridership had increased greatly and there was interest in purchasing Harley Davidson motorcycles. However, many thought that the organization should address some of the key concerns of diversity before entering the HD family. There were many polled in the study that felt HD was not interested in the additional customers because of a variety of their experiences within the dealer network. *(HD did work with the dealer network to address many concerns that had been felt by many of its minority customers.)* The chairman thought my study was a great idea, but suggested that I work with other leaders in the organization to foster buy-in and not force the initiative on the company. The importance of this study and the need for new riders was not seen as a priority and the importance of the project was diluted by the other leaders due to the current successes we were experiencing. There have been tremendous efforts by HD over the years to increase its customer base by becoming more engaging in new or different markets domestically as well as internationally.

I am in no way criticizing Harley Davidson for what it did not do or should have done. However, I believe that if a holistic strategy were done in conjunction with true current state assessments it would have produced results that should have changed some of the unfortunate conditions of today. Today, there is a tremendous amount of inventory left at the dealerships, layoffs of employees, and people leaving the company. Because much of the waste was built into the processes and capacity increases during the growth of the company, the staffing levels and spending had far exceeded the balance with sales levels. While economic conditions also had an impact on the company, a holistic strategy, current state understanding, and having a stronger pulse on the customer would have lessened this blow.

There has been a change in the operating structure from a circle leadership structure to a more traditional leadership structure. This appeared to be a reaction or solution to the changes in the marketplace, shortfall of revenues, or possibly it was seen as a Silver Bullet. This change kept much of the same leadership, with the same skill sets that got the organization in the current state it is in. However, operating within a new structure they were unfamiliar with. This type of reaction may happen more often than not in organizations that seek a Silver Bullet during impactful financial times. There has been a change in the marketplace; however, we knew that the riders were aging, and there was a potential for the market to change years ago. I love Harley Davidson, but without great planning, I believe we were no different than many other companies. Good during the good or profitable times and then scrambling during tough times. An eye on the current state could have helped this situation.

Another example of not wanting to understand the current state of the business was something I experienced during my time as Vice President at Ingersoll Rand. There was clear communication amongst the leadership of the company of the intent to grow the organization from $10 to $20B. The vision or three key drivers from the CEO were:

1. Operational Excellence
2. Dual Citizenship
3. Dramatic Growth

These words were constantly communicated but very little was done in regards to either looking at how this growth would be achieved, or what the current state of the business looked like.

There were financial commitments and plans to support the growth but the infrastructure to support it was not in place. This organization was over four times the size of Harley Davidson and had a huge global presence with over 44,000 employees. The interesting part about Ingersoll Rand was that it was made up of a variety of acquisitions and was experiencing a tremendous amount of change. The need for an overall strategy, or holistic strategy, and an understanding of the current state of the business/business unit was tremendous. Because of the makeup of this organization, with the number of acquisitions that comprised the company, it was even more important to have a sound integration process and common metrics that would provide a sense of control and unity across the organization. This failure in planning was complicated by the fact that there was a significant amount of employee turnover at all levels, the processes and systems were poorly thought out, and the needed level of sophistication from leadership was a daunting prospect. There were clear signs of the intent to grow the organization and to appease the Wall Street analysts with the financial numbers. Every sector had the appearance of great financial plans to achieve these aggressive goals, but the organization was looking for a Silver Bullet in the form of operational excellence to help deliver the results. The commitment to operational excellence was equivalent to the condition of the overall corporate strategy, nonexistent to poor at best. There were expectations to reduce cost throughout the organization, but very few definable execution plans. With the conditions of the organization and the void of a real corporate plan or a holistic strategy, the operational excellence initiative was nothing more than a window dressing that was doomed to fail. The current state of the business was never assessed as the organization forged on with its growth plans. The huge turnover throughout the company, which in and of itself would present a challenge of building and maintaining competencies while growing, was never addressed. The sophistication of leadership and its ability to launch a strategy even within the strongest sectors was a weakness. The state of engineering, supply chain, and operations was dismal. Common metrics, plant layouts, financial reporting systems, voids in many policies, broken processes in the transactional areas (HR, Finance, IT, etc) and the lack of turnaround experience or talent were a few specific issues that needed to also be corrected.

If there had been, at the very least, an effort to look at the current state of the organization within the sectors, I am sure that the "how to" questions would have impacted the thoughts and planning of the anticipated pace of growth.

As part of the team that was attempting to create a business operating system and the leader of Operational Excellence for one of the company's largest sectors, there were many challenges I faced. The lack of a corporate strategy and the resources necessary to begin looking at the current state of the business was one of the biggest. We had a seasoned leader heading the efforts for operational excellence in the company, but he was trying to do this without the direct support of most of the sector presidents. Other than this one leader, most of the operational excellence team members had never operated at the strategic level of any organization, and some not even at the operational level. The master black belts and black belt competencies that were present were important but could not be substituted for leadership experience. After a number of attempts to help the organization understand what would be needed to ensure that operational excellence would be a viable tool, a change in staffing was made and the new operational excellence leader, a veteran of the organization nearing retirement, but with minimal operational excellence exposure, was brought in to smooth the ruffled feathers. The chairman hoped for success of the operational excellence program but was not willing to provide the level of support or the commitment needed for it to succeed, another story of time in grade and a Silver Bullet exemplifying the lack of serious commitment to change from the senior leadership.

After assessing my sector, I attempted to establish a current state with the expectations of helping to ensure we could build a sound strategy to succeed in our growth plans. Although the strategy should be completed first, I focused on what I could influence. I developed a simple process that we will discuss in the next chapter. This process involved leadership in a few of the areas of the business, including the largest business unit within the nearly $2B sector, human resources, finance, engineering and the aftermarket business. Almost all of the sessions were productive and produced a clear picture of the current state they were in, where the organization was going, how it was to get there, a roadmap, metrics, communications plan, and accountability. (Again, all of this process is discussed in the strategy matrix portion of this book.)

After we had spent a week developing this process, and generated a lot of excitement amongst the teams, for knowing what was going on, we ran into a huge challenge: resources were needed that had never been allocated. The challenges were evident in each area of the $1.3B business unit, the one that was to provide the largest part of the corporation's growth. Resources were needed to establish a true voice of the customer, develop the acquisition pipeline and process, streamline new product development to focus on the customer wants, etc. HR needed resources to help reduce the turnover problem by developing effective recruiting and retention programs, succession planning and evaluation processes. Finance needed resources, engineering needed resources, and the aftermarket needed resources. The sales channels needed a great deal of structure and accountability so that they were more closely aligned with the rest of the business units and the customers. The need to drive for additional resources was systemic because the growth initiatives had been established without an understanding of the current state of these areas and the inherent needs of that state. In many instances, talent was needed just to do the assessment, to understand what was needed, and to accomplish what was being asked.

As I continued through my process, it became clear that where the organization was expecting to be and where the business units actually were at were not even close. There was a huge gap in place. It seemed as though most of the people knew that there were problems with the direction, but did not want to discuss it because of some sort of fear. This fear or reluctance to address the problems mixed with a hope that suggested that the purpose of the operational excellence initiative was to come in and close the gap for the leaders. This way they could be successful without ever having to deal with the problem. This was definitely the hope for a Silver Bullet fix. The company failed in communicating operational excellence as a paradigm shift in the way a business operates by the lack of provisional resources and its overall commitment to the process.

As I began to discuss the outcomes of my current state planning, assessments and solutions with other senior leaders, it became clear that nothing different was going to be done. It was also clear that the sector vision of doubling revenues in 5 years (including acquisitions), of achieving at least 15% operating income in all business cycles, and generating at least 25% return on invested capital all at the same time would be a virtually impossible challenge with this mindset. These goals and statements of vision are great "pie in the sky" words that excited Wall Street, but without a plan or holistic strategy supporting the vision that included a clear understanding of the current state, these words might as well be written in the sand on the beach.

As with Harley Davidson, I am not trying to be critical of the issues and how they came about at Ingersoll Rand, I am trying to make the point that a clear unbiased development of the current state would have revealed a significant decision point for the senior leadership. They would have been able to consider their plans in light of the current state of the business and either keep going with the understanding that it would be tough to make the goals that had been committed to Wall Street or to address those conditions shown in the current state, which in this case would have been costly. Whether they decided to change the growth expectations of Wall Street or the cost to achieve them, it would impact the stock price. Either way the focus would have had a short term or longer term impact on Wall Street and the company's shareholders because the objectives could not be met unless something was done differently.

My experiences in the home building industry were not much different. The vision was to buy land and build homes the fastest way they knew how, thereby growing revenues. It was another love child industry of Wall Street. There were never any real strategies, execution plans, or understanding of the current state on the radar. There was not a true understanding of how much it actually cost to build a home, and the only thought was to pass the cost (inflation, wastes, etc.) to the homebuyer without negatively impacting revenues.

As we get into the body of this section, we will look at what is required to understand the current state of the business or business unit and how to create one. It is a very sensitive topic because it exposes a lot of weaknesses and problems within the organization. It exposes process problems, competency issues, and resource needs and could expose some financial reporting issues that are separate from the actual workings of the business. As Toyota looks at problems within its organization as positives and opportunities to be fixed, we must accept the current state of any business as just such an opportunity.

I would suggest that whether you are looking at an entire organization or a business unit/function, the important part of understanding the current state is to spend the time and effort to do an accurate assessment. An effective approach to this process is to focus on people, processes and systems.

People

As we begin to look at establishing a current state for the people in the organization, you must begin with the most senior leader of that organization. Whether it is the CEO of a large corporation or an owner of a small company, the beginning of this process must be with the top. You must take a critical look at this individual and get a clear unbiased assessment as to the strengths and weaknesses of the individual, what that person does extremely well, what they do not do as well, or needs improvement in, and how the person got to the level they are at. This is important to know so that you can understand whether the person earned their way to the top or was handed the keys to the ship and was not a proven leader. Is this person performance based, relationship based, or a combination of both? Is this person clear about the roles and responsibilities as defined in the leadership portion of this book?   There are many other questions you might ask as part of the assessment.

1. How effective have they been in the past, setting a vision, mission and strategy? Was it all encompassing or was it a financial plan?
2. How will they assess the current staff and the organization?
3. How will they get and receive feedback?
4. How will success be measured?
5. How will decisions be made?
6. How and what businesses information will be communicated and when?

It will also be important to understand the person's business acumen and what experience they have in different parts of the business. Many companies focus on hiring leaders from the financial areas, because of their financial experience, and some from engineering, because of their technical experience. Some come from the sales/marketing disciplines. It is ironic that although all of these disciplines have significant impact on the product, this is not necessarily where the process skills are. When you look at the process and process innovation in these particular areas, they are not historically the leaders of change. The importance of understanding these items at the senior level is because that is where the recruiting process needs to begin. As the vision and strategy is being developed, ensuring that you have the right people on the team is critical. The balance of the executive level staff should be based on an assessment of the talents and weaknesses of the leader. If the leader is weak in a particular area, he/she should ensure that the strength of one of his/her staff compensates for their weakness. A leader with a strong financial background should ensure that they have a strong sales/marketing leader and, depending on the type of business, a strong engineering, operations, or supply chain person as key leaders of the business. Having most of the makeup of the leadership team from one discipline can cause potential problems. As you look at the technical skills of the senior staff, it is also important to look at their soft skills. Is the leader a type-A personality? If so, you might wish to create a balance with the personality of the next in charge or the executive staff. With this process beginning at the top, the process from the leader and the senior staff should cascade throughout the organization. The recruiting, retention, and succession planning initiatives should be part of the strategy and begin at this level with the strengths and weaknesses of everyone throughout the organization.

I have seen plenty of recruiting processes that focused on how the hiring manager felt about a candidate. Without a clear strategy, this will yield mixed results. People will tend to hire those much like themselves or those that seem to get along best with the hiring managers instead of getting the most qualified candidate. Instead, the hiring process should focus on the strengths and weaknesses of the organization and needs based on the plan or holistic strategy. If the alignment of this process is in place, favoritism, cronyism, and many of the diversity issues we face within organizations would be greatly diminished. As you pass down through the leadership continuum and get to the tactical or direct levels from the strategic and operational levels, the focus will shift from staff makeup to where individual skills will become more important.

As you look at the people within your organization, you will have to look at the effectiveness of the competency development in training programs, evaluation systems, compensation, communication methods, and the involvement and engagement of the employees. Looking at each of these areas that human resources typically manages, you will need to ensure that they are part of the strategic plan, and that the following questions are asked of each:

1. What is the current state of each of these areas? Are they working well?
2. What is not working well with each?
3. Where, as part of the strategy, do you intend these to be in the future?

In the subsequent strategic matrix planning portion of this book, we use a 3-year evaluation because it looks far enough into the future, but is close enough, to the present, to ensure actions are taken to achieve the goals.

With the fact that people or human capital are always the most important asset a company possesses, and having the right people on the team and leadership that is effective, there is not much that a company cannot achieve successfully.

Process

In this portion, the current state of process, we will begin to look at the importance in having great processes throughout your organization. Whether in a large company or a small business, every function of a business that involves getting a product or service to a customer can be considered as utilizing a process. The biggest challenge of understanding the current state of processes is knowing your customer, their expectations, and needs. As you understand your customer's needs, you **MUST** understand how your processes are currently operating and how effective or ineffective they are being performed. This is important for businesses, whether they provide a product or a service. Every process within an organization needs to be measured in some form. This helps to establish an environment of accountability. As we begin to focus on managing the process, there are eight key items we should remember:

- Managing should be to a set of matrices and not anecdotal feelings.
- Accountability of personnel will be adherence to the defined process.
- Training and buy-in to any and all processes should be the norm.
- Everyone should know what is expected of them and trained on how to achieve and be successful within the matrix driven workplace.
- There should be no surprises, only known outcomes.
- There is no management of a process without measurement.
- Strategy and tactics will be the method of running the business.
- And most of all, understanding the customers' needs shall drive all of the above.

Remembering these keys will help as you begin to look at your processes and while preparing your strategy. As you remember these keys, we will look at the 8 types of waste that can occur within your organization; these are present in almost every function of every company, so you must look out for them. We will look at eliminating waste later in this chapter.

But Why?

Those of us that have kids or have been around them have heard children ask "but why?" as a never-ending series of questions. This sometimes annoying barrage of questions is kids trying to learn from their experiences and their parents. This is really a wonderful tool that we can all use in our everyday lives and can help us to get to the root cause of problems instead of looking for quick fixes or Silver Bullets. This process is as simple as it is useful. An example would be:

Q. Why did we miss the scheduled delivery to our customer?
A. We did not have all of the necessary parts.

Q. Why didn't we have the necessary parts?
A. They were late coming from the supplier.

Q. Why were they late coming from the supplier?
A. Joe did not order them on time.

Q. Why didn't Joe order them on time?
A. He was on vacation

Q. Why was Joe on vacation and no one was assigned to cover his duties?

This is an example that yielded two obvious problems that might have never been addressed had it not been for the five why process. First, in a lean system or pull environment a kanban would have been set up with a trigger that the operator would have noticed prior to the shortage. The other problem that needed to be addressed was that the operation had a good system to ensure that prior to Joe leaving for vacation that there was proper coverage to ensure that the TAKT times would not be impacted by parts shortages. In this scenario, the root cause of the customer's expectations was not met because Joe went on vacation without coverage for his parts. A kanban system could have helped prevent this problem as well.

At Toyota, the practice of 'five why's' used as a series of questions is also used to get to the root cause of many problems throughout the organization. Much of the Toyota production system has been built on this approach. Because at Toyota they believe in actually solving problems, and eliminating waste, this tool has become very helpful. The approach is to ask why five times and answering it each time. This is believed to get to the root cause of problems, which are often hidden behind more obvious symptoms. There may be times when getting to the fifth why will be tough; however, taking the time to complete the process can make the difference between truly eliminating a problem and instituting a Silver Bullet. This is the scientific basis of the Toyota system. Just like taking the time to answer these questions from kids can help them to learn and understand why, incorporating this type of process in a company can help it to eliminate problems and learn more effectively.

Eliminating Waste

In every process, regardless of business or industry, there are two types of activities. These are value added activities, which are activities that transform raw materials or information to meet or exceed customer expectations. There is also non value added activities, which are the activities in a process that takes time, resources, or occupy space but do not contribute to the value of a product or service. The key to any process improvement activities is to define these two items and eliminate the wastes within. It is these wastes that impacts a company's bottom line and will increase the cost of a product or service. Having the right people on the team is key, but then ensuring that the people have effective processes and are working in the most efficient manner possible is good for any business. There are eight general types of wastes that are a part of these activities you need to watch for:

1. **Overproduction -** producing more than the customer (internal or external) wants or needs.
2. **Waiting -** anyone waiting for a product, service, or next action to occur throughout a process.
3. **Transportation -** moving products or services throughout a process that are not needed. How is the process laid out?

4. **Processing -** providing or duplicating more paperwork, trans-
    actions or activities needed throughout a process. Reduce
    what you do not need and standardize when possible.
5. **Unnecessary motions -** within a process, cell or function,
    any movement to achieve activity that is not needed.
6. **Inventory or stock -** accumulating parts, paperwork or trans-
    actions in excess of what is needed to meet a production or
    service goal for the customer.
7. **Defective goods or bad services -** poor quality requiring
    repair, rework, or return to fix a problem.
8. **People -** failure to properly allocate, utilize or motivate per-
    sonnel is one of the greatest wastes. It is created through inef-
    fective leadership, lack of vision and strategy, and
    accountability by metrics.

As you look at the types of activities we have discussed, value
and non value added, and seek out the eight wastes within your organization, you will begin to see the tremendous amount of opportunity. This should also be a part of the information gathered as the
current state of the business becomes defined. You should remember
that the process of identifying the current state should be revisited
frequently. I have used this process annually, and that has worked
well for me. Organizations focus on many of these process activities
within the manufacturing areas; however, this can work in every area
of every company. I have seen the financial impact of identifying and
addressing the eight wastes in many non value added activities and
areas such as human resources, engineering, finance, and supply
chain can be larger than in the operations areas. Remember, all of
these areas have frontline positions that impact business revenues as
well. Whether it is poor recruiting processes, the time it takes to complete an engineering drawing, or the time needed to complete the
necessary transactions for monthly reporting and payroll, it is all
waste that equates to lost revenues. A culture of openness will allow
people to look at all waste as non value added activities that are
opportunities for improvement.

As lost revenues add up, because of poor processes, some
organizations such as Toyota use a different perspective. They focus
on value add and non value add within their processes as part of their

fundamentals, focusing diligently on how things are being done and the processes to help the overall organization. They look for the problems and issues throughout their company as opportunities to solve. One of Toyota's first fundamentals is using a *non-cost principle.*

Instead of the manufacturer determining the selling price by using a formula of cost to manufacture product + profit = selling price. They use a formula of selling price – (minus) cost to manufacture = profit. Toyota understands that the customer or the market determines the selling price and not the costs of accumulative non value processes in the factory.

This "non cost principle" sounds counter-intuitive until you look at it as a process of determining selling price based on the customer. This shift in thinking allows you to build the value of the product first and hence the sales and marketing concept before establishing the price point. It reduces the chance of bringing a product to market that is overpriced for its perceived value. It also serves to highlight potential profitability problems so that steps can be taken to reduce the built-in costs prior to a launch rather than after, when you are bleeding red ink.

Toyota also understands that only good processes add value, all other operations such as quality inspectors, transport of parts, waiting, etc. adds no value to the product itself. They work diligently to eliminate as many non value operations as possible. They believe there is no such thing as an improvement in a non value operation, period. In this method, you must understand your processes, the non value added activities and the value added activities. You should also understand and identify the waste that is occurring in each of your processes throughout your organization. There are probably a handful of companies that utilize this method of thinking. The others are looking for a Silver Bullet or some other form of hope to become successful.

If you reviewed the change in accounting philosophy that I suggested in Chapter 6, you will find that this non-cost way of thinking is complimentary to the lean accounting philosophy. Our traditional way of accounting and the thought of finance driving the organization is probably a huge contributor to our current state of affairs and search for Silver Bullet fixes, and why Toyota is experiencing so much of the successes that it has.

SYSTEMS

It seems that most people think of systems as Information Technology; however, systems link everything together within an organization. Everything is a system, every system is part of a larger system, and every system is comprised of smaller systems. This includes the company's informational operating system, but that is not all. It is the common thread of communication, metrics, financials, delivery schedules, engineering, sales, supply chain, and human resources. It is the way the business operates, an integration of how things function as a whole. How the vision and strategy are executed can be considered a system. As you look at the processes and the current state, you must understand what you need out of a business operating system, your information systems and reporting systems. You will want to take an inventory of all of the different systems you have in your organization and begin to assess them.

1. How are they working?
2. Are you getting information that you need across the organization?
3. If you are, how is this being communicated?
4. How effective are the systems?
5. How are they being measured?

Some organizations again look for a Silver Bullet such as SAP, Oracle, or other operating systems to solve all of their organization issues.

The successful application of any system requires good leadership, a sound strategy, understanding of the current state, and knowing your customer. If your need is to explore an operating system for much of your information handling, it is a good idea to have a clear plan and have as much information as possible standardized before you attempt a switch. This will reduce the amount of variability being inputted into the new system. It is also important to know what you want versus what you need and how much the system will cost. The actual value of the type of system you are seeking is a critical component. It will help to ensure you are not paying for more than you may need or over-engineering a system for your business needs. I have been a part of a few system implementations where what we wanted and what was interpreted by the software leaders had a gap. This gap normally occurs between the operating unit or customer and the designer of the software. In my experience there is sometimes a communication gap over terminology or what may be perceived as needed or wanted. This gap will often prove to be costly and the implementation learning curve steeper. An integrator will often be helpful. An integrator is someone that has a good grasp of your business or strong business acumen and knows the capabilities of various software applications. Normally software providers will provide someone like this, however their focus will be to sell the software of the provider that they are working with which maybe not to the best interest of your business. If you are looking at changing your business operating system, this should be predicated on your vision and strategy, and not as a separate initiative that may actually be in conflict with them. Understanding the current state of your systems throughout the organization is crucial to your execution plans within your strategy.

Measurements and Accountability

All processes must and should be measured. This includes people, processes and systems. All processes are a part of the operational DNA of every function within a company or business. This DNA can be referred to as the company operating system. Whether this is formalized through a process with a house and pillars like Toyota, or the business process at Harley Davidson, it is still a system. The effectiveness of how every function works together, to meet or exceed customer's expectations, through integration of people and processes will define how smoothly the company's systems are coordinating and how well it executes its strategy and achieves its vision.

In this section, we have looked at the two types of activities, value added and non value added. We have reviewed the eight types of waste, and provided some clarity for the requirements within people, process and systems. It is clear that each of these areas must be measured. As you look at all aspects of leading an organization, you will need to be able to assess them. You will need to have assessments for your people, for your processes and every system within the organization. These assessments will define the current state in each of these areas and this will ensure that what the leader is planning within the vision and strategy the organization will be equipped with the tools necessary for success. As you begin to assess your people, the leader will have to be confident that you have a good understanding of what the strengths and weaknesses are for each group and most people in the organization. This will be very helpful to the organization in a variety of ways, including succession planning, the recruiting process, and, most importantly, the clear strengths and weaknesses of the organization as a whole. Having a vision and strategy without the people with the skill sets required to achieve the tasks is the same as not having the proper equipment. Although the assessments of your people may not tell you everything, they can be a helpful resource to understand what can be accomplished and what kind of bench strength you have. There are assessment tools available that deal with personality style, soft skills, technical skills, and organizational fit, whether you choose off-the-shelf tools or have one built for the needs of the organization, do what will best prepare the team for success.

There are lean assessments and a variety of other types of assessments that can help to understand how effective your processes are across the organization. The lean assessments are a good tool to help understand whether you have effective processes, and can provide a streamlined system of activities that will provide solutions if you need some additional support. These assessments can help to identify how organized your business is, how much waste you have within the organization from the 8 wastes), and whether you have the right number of people, layout, and maintenance systems for your equipment. The focus of the lean assessment is to eliminate the non value added activities within all processes in the organization.

In this chapter, we have discussed the importance of identifying the current state of your business and getting a good sense of the systems you have within your organization and how effective they are. The keys to understanding the condition of your business must include every facet of your operation. Identifying what is value added and non value added in every function is important. Utilizing the 8 wastes will be a good tool to start understanding the value added and non value added activities within your organization. As you begin to focus on the current state, you will start to understand the expectations of the people and processes within your systems. If you do not understand the current state of your entire business, you cannot see the strengths that will allow you to forge ahead and the weaknesses that can cause you to stumble. This failure can and will have a significant impact to the overall effectiveness of your vision and strategy. Without this, I am not sure how effective the organization can be.

As in the examples I provided from my experiences at Harley Davidson, Ingersoll Rand, and Pulte, I have shown that a better understanding of the current state of the organization would have produced different results. The current state establishes a starting point or baseline for where an organization is at a given time. In each of these cases, understanding the current state would have changed the expectations of the strategy, and may have ultimately had some impact on the vision of each. Often establishing a current state, as in developing an all-encompassing plan or holistic strategy, will take time and cost money. The money invested in this part of the business is a clear investment in the long-term viability of the organization, and part of the responsibility of a leader of any organization.

Without the preparation of these activities, any unexpected change in the markets or leadership is an iceberg in the path of the Titanic, and the organization's people and all its programs and projects will be impacted. It is important to remember that hope is not a process. Hoping something gets accomplished in the organization without effective processes to facilitate it is a dangerous dream. Understanding the current state of your organization will reduce the need to *hope* that things will get accomplished, and you will begin to understand how it is possible to confidently *expect* that your plans will succeed.

3-YEAR STRATEGY MATRIX PROCESS

As we have begun to look at the complex process of building a strategy, I wanted to provide a tool that I have used during my career. This is a simple tool that is geared to help any leadership team at any level to put together a plan that will help them get from their current state out 3 years. I use 3 years because it is far enough away from the day of the event to allow for significant change and growth, but close enough to create a sense of urgency the day after the planning session. This process should not and cannot replace the holistic strategy process, but it will provide a level of tactical direction in the absence of one or during the development of one. The most effective way for implementation of this process is to begin at the strategic or senior level of leadership. Because there are so many organizations that have not implemented a thorough or holistic strategy company wide, this process can be done at operational and direct levels to establish direction and alignment for its team members and provide a baseline proof of the system for the whole of the organization. I would normally only recommend that this is done at the operational or direct levels if there is not much support from the strategic level. While it can at least align everyone at these levels, there is a risk that there may be a misalignment with the support functions that support your group and again at the strategic level. This will usually create challenges and the strategic planning tool tends to be sub optimized. For proactive leaders, this can be another opportunity that may be a great tool to use to manage upward. It will show how you are aligning the levels that you might have influence with and how the tool can be helpful to the wider organization. Again, all this can be useful and the risk is in the overall alignment with the rest of the value stream. Many of the customers within the rest of the value stream may have different objectives and being in alignment with your function may not be a priority for them.

The 3-year strategy matrix has some similarities with Toyota's A3 report and I expect with many others. However, this streamlined process has worked well for me. This process includes a current state view by the entire leadership team (at the level it is being implemented) and a 3-year strategic tool. It also includes:

1. A roadmap to show how the team will get from where they are to where they are going.
2. A 30-, 60-, 90-day plan that will ensure that immediate action.
3. Metrics are created for all areas.
4. A communication plan to all employees is defined.
5. A plan for meeting expectations, times and frequency (daily, weekly, monthly and quarterly).
6. An accountability report geared to begin actions the day after the event.

Value stream mapping (VSM) is also very useful and is an outstanding tool that will compliment the strategy matrix. I have utilized this strategy matrix and other strategic tools prior to implementing the VSM because it provides an initial direction and will align the leadership of the teams in the continuum to a common understanding of the current state of the organization. The VSM focuses on the flow and conditions of the processes. The VSM and strategy matrix complement each other in developing a clear understanding of the current state of the organization.

Developing the Strategy Matrix

The Strategic Matrix development includes a roadmap that will further dissect the activities and timelines required to achieve the vision and strategy as committed on the matrix itself. There is also a 30-, 60-, 90-day plan that will ensure that immediate action to achieve the desired results of the strategy matrix are started immediately following the session. Accountability is defined through metrics created during this time and champions for each activity are assigned. Meeting times, frequency of meetings (daily, weekly, monthly, and quarterly) and communication to all employees is also defined during this time.

This process normally takes a few days and involves leadership representation from each applicable function as it relates to the level. This process can be completed on five pieces of paper, usually in graph format. As President, I included my entire staff of direct reports. In other functional roles, I included the leadership representatives of the customers that we served or as suppliers served my team. During my tenure at Harley Davidson, this included the union leadership. They were involved in almost all aspects of leadership projects that I led. It is absolutely essential that each function is represented at each level during this process because the dialogue that occurs during the current state portion of the strategy matrix is priceless. This will also ensure that an alignment as to the vision of where the team is going is understood and "buy-in" is achieved. In every session I have led using a strategy matrix or a derivative program, it is the current state process that creates the most passion and really ends up opening the eyes of the leaders. It opens their eyes because they often do not know the impact of problems from their customers or effects their actions were causing. The scope of the items that are covered during the current state should not be excessive, but should be representative of the organization's issues of what is working well and what is not working well.

After the team agrees on the current state, the next step is to begin to identify the direction of change or the 3-year objectives. As the entire team is now in agreement and has bought into the current state of the business, managing expectations of where they can go over the next 3 years is the next hurdle. It is such because this step begins to challenge the commitment of the organization with regards to resources, equipment, funding and priorities. The 3-year objectives should not encompass more than five or six objectives in each of the five to seven headers or titles of the categories on the top of the strategy matrix.

Once the team identifies its 3-year objectives, the next challenge becomes year 1. Year 1 begins the bridge process from the current state and what it will require to ensure success of the 3-year objectives. It is essential that every issue identified during the current state, especially the broken processes, are addressed during this step. Each of these issues will need to be addressed in the plan for the year-1 through -3 of the process. In some instances, because of the size and scope of an issue, it may take longer than 3 years to fix, but it should be addressed through some activities over the next 3 years or shelved for a later date. Year 2 of the matrix acts as a bridge for activities between years 1 and 3 and provides the continuity of purpose and direction to ensure success. (See example of a strategy matrix in Appendix A)

The Road Map

The roadmap process covers each activity listed in year 1 of the strategy matrix. Each activity is discussed by the team and the items required to accomplish the activities of year 1 are placed in each of the year's quarters. Each goal for year 1 is dissected and the activities that are assigned to complete the task are added into each quarter of the roadmap. The activities may also be allocated throughout the year and have their respective tasks needed to support the goal recorded in each respective quarter. An example of this would be if the team is working to improve their Talent Acquisition as a 3-year strategy. The year-1 focus is to implement behavioral interviewing and the following example may be a part of the roadmap process.

- Quarter 1, train the HR team in behavioral interviewing.
- Quarter 2, train the appropriate leadership in same.
- Quarter 3, begin behavioral interviewing process. Also, continue training other members that will be a part of the process.
- Quarter 4, may have a certain percentage of a company, business unit or function trained.

Depending on the size of the organization, this may continue into year 2. As you begin this process, there may be modifications to the roadmap due to organizational constraints, but changes should be agreed upon by the team that developed it. I cannot stress enough the importance of the details in the roadmap. If there are issues in year 1 of the strategy matrix that are not represented by action items in the roadmap, it is almost a certainty that the goals will not be achieved for year 1, thereby setting up the team for failure. This type of situation can be alleviated or avoided with a properly developed strategy matrix that includes a review process, thereby identifying the needed for modification of the roadmap. Having Leadership team members assigned as Champions to each activity ensures accountability of the process and removal of barriers during the execution of the activities of the roadmap. (See example of Road map in Appendix)

The 30-, 60-, 90-Day Plan of Action

The 30-, 60-, 90-day plan is a further breakdown of the requirements during each quarter of the roadmap that will ensure timelines are met and goals are achieved. The development of these action plans follows the same general pattern as the roadmap, but they get down to more of the nitty gritty details and specific tasks that are needed to realize the quarterly, yearly and long-term goals. The structure of the Strategy Matrix, Roadmap, and 30,- 60-, 90-Day plan of action follows the same pattern we discussed in the leadership section of the book. This pattern is the hierarchy of Strategic, Tactical and Operational, and it is this integration and permeation of these essential concepts throughout all aspects of an organization that can help to stack the odds in the favor of your success. (See example of the 30-, 60-, 90-day plan in Appendix).

Engagement of All

During part four of the process, metrics will need to be created and defined. As we have previously discussed, we must measure our activities and progress through metrics to ensure accountability that the overall vision and strategy goals are met. The core metrics should be cost, quality and delivery, and they need to be consistent with the other metrics within the organization. This commonality of metrics to the overall organization ensures clear understandability and accountability within the strategy matrix by the entire team. This accountability must be tied to performance review and to the compensation of individuals in the company in exactly the same way it should be incorporated as a portion of the overall strategy of the company.

As a part of the overall Engagement plan, communication and meetings should also be defined. What will be communicated daily, weekly, monthly, quarterly and annually? A plan for who should attend meetings and what should be covered will prevent confusion and wasted time. It is important to ensure that all employees understand where the organization is going, and frequent, focused meetings should be a part of the process. These will help keep people engaged, excited and afford them the opportunity to offer suggestions and ideas that can open the door to more successes. (See example of the Communication plan in Appendix)

The Parking Lot

This portion can be called almost anything, and has often been referred to as a 'follow-up items' or 'to be determined' list. It is the area where items that need resolution but are not on the immediate action list are stored so that they are revisited for action at a later time and not forgotten. This list should be assigned owners so that the open items can be reviewed periodically during the meetings and their status assessed for potential impact and action.

As you can see, the 3-Year Strategy Matrix process should be in support of the overall vision and strategy of the organization, business or business unit. It is important that leaders throughout the leadership continuum and at every level participate in the process. This process ensures that the strategy has a foundation, that it is in alignment with the vision, and that the strategy has accountability tied to it.

The Value Stream Mapping (VSM) process works well with the 3-Year Strategy Matrix. It is imperative to understand how the parts of the organization are interrelated, and how each function supports the next. I usually implement that VSM process after this portion, so that there is some sense of direction and alignment for the teams. In most of my experiences we did not have a holistic or thorough strategic planning process, so this was how I decided to proceed. In some instances it might be better to complete the VSM process first. It could be of benefit in understanding the flow of the organization, and potential bottlenecks prior to moving into the Strategy Matrix process.

Value Stream Mapping will also be covered in the next section in more detail, but **VSM** is a lean technique used to analyze the flow of materials and information currently required to bring a product or service to a consumer. At Toyota, where the technique originated, it is known as "Material and Information Flow Mapping." Although VSM is often associated with manufacturing, it is also used in logistics, supply chain, service-related industries, software development and product development. As a general overview the implementation process for VSM is as follows:

1. Identify the target product, product family, or service.
2. Draw a current state value stream map, which is the current steps, delays, and information flows required to deliver the target product or service. This may be a production flow (raw materials to consumer) or a design flow (concept to launch). There are 'standard' symbols for representing supply chain entities.
3. Assess the current state value stream map in terms of creating flow by eliminating waste.
4. Draw a future state value stream map.
5. Implement the future state.
6. Design the ideal state.

INSTITUTING CHANGE

<u>There is nothing more difficult to plan, more doubtful of success, nor more dangerous to manage than the creation of a new order of things.....</u>
Niccolo Machiavelli, 1513

We have reviewed leadership and the roles and responsibilities of leaders and developing a vision/mission and strategy, and now we will look at the process of creating or transforming a system. This is one of the most challenging parts of running a business. In the other parts that we have discussed, involvement was largely centered on the leadership and what its roles and responsibilities are. In this portion, the entire organization is involved in the change or transformation process. In an existing organization, this process can be very complex and challenging. In a start-up organization it can set the tone of how the business will be run, but the changes here can be just as great because it can be a matter of changing mindsets.

Everyone knows that change can be difficult, but is a part of our lives. Just like the two things that are a guarantee in our lives, death and paying taxes, change is a constant. Most of us experience change every day of our lives. Change is most difficult when it involves changing our lives and the way we perceive things, our beliefs. As we know, our lives are governed by three factors: genetics, environment, and experiences. These three inputs shape the way we actually think about things and conceptually see them. It often requires a great deal of re-education to change the way somebody thinks or does things. Changing a business, or any of its constituent parts and functions, is not much different. It will require a great deal of re-education of the thinking processes and the way we do our work within a business. In many cases, the business operating culture will need to be transformed, and this type of situation involves introducing change into many people's lives. This brings with it an elevated level of stress that leaders must deal with for the change to be effective. We all experience change personally, professionally, or even as a society. You may experience change personally with finances, marriages, weather, health, death of a family member, or just growing older. Professionally, you may experience change by getting a promotion, a raise, a new job, a new career or even a lay-off. Societal changes can impact us personally, professionally or both, and it can occur due to seasons, war, the economy, or because of technological advances. Refusal to change can be extremely detrimental in each of these or any situation.

An example of societal change that we did not learn from was the Vietnam War. We had not changed our military tactics from World War II and the Korean War prior to the Vietnam War. Fighting a war in a theater of steaming jungles when we were not prepared caused many casualties, and the many disabled military personnel from that war have affected many families today. In the same way, as we ventured into the global war on terrorism, our preparation and training was hampered because we were still primarily training to support combat in the climates of Europe and Southeast Asia and not a war in the dessert of Iraq and the mountains of Afghanistan.

Again, the failure and refusal to learn about change in war is causing many unnecessary casualties. The business world is exactly the same, as the customers change and the economy changes, so must the way we do business. A failure or refusal to change the way you do business will result in another type of casualty. These casualties will be the continued loss of businesses, loss of jobs, and layoffs of employees that we are seeing with greater frequency every day.

THE BUSINESS OPERATING SYSTEM

Whether you have a 50-year-old company or are planning to start a new company, having a business operating system (BOS) is a critical component to your success. A BOS is the common structure, principles and practices necessary to drive the entire organization. A BOS does this by creating repeatable processes and sustainable performance in support of the vision/mission and strategy. The BOS encompasses the leadership continuum, as well as every business unit and functional area of the company. This is important to know because, much like the strategy and vision, the BOS involves the entire company and cannot be delegated. To develop, design or implement a BOS below the strategic level of leadership within the organization is a recipe for failure. I am not suggesting that the lower levels should not be involved, however, the ownership, frameworks and accountability must be held at the strategic level of the organization for it to be successful. This process is important to the success of the organization, and depending on the size of the organization, it may take quite a bit of time and effort. Many companies are scrambling to build business operating systems or business processes that mirror Toyota's "house and pillars." In many instances, the BOS is being created as another Silver Bullet, with the hopes that creating a structured system within the organization will cure all of its ills. A BOS should be used as a supporting tool of the strategic plan. It is a tool that helps define the parameters of "how" the organization will operate. It is geared to help an organization meet the customer's expectations.

The BOS helps to ensure that the key metrics needed to meet the customer's expectations (delivering the product or service when the customer wants it, at the fit and form or quality the customer expects, and at a cost they are willing to pay). The BOS must also encompass your supplier interface, how they are a part of your system, and how employees will be empowered and held accountable through measures in every function of your company. An example of the components of a BOS is:

1. Process Management - includes how the overall strategy will be deployed and how the vision will be met.
2. Operational Excellence - includes lean and six sigma tools for holistic usage across the organization.
3. Communication Plan - how, when and what the organization will communicate and to whom.
4. People and Culture - how this will be established and what it should function like.
5. Growth - methods and functional plans in support of the vision and supply chain (Sales, Inventory, and Operations Planning (SIOP), Supplier Development, Supply Base and Commodity Management).

These are examples of what is in a BOS; however, depending on the organization, the size and scope may vary to support the needs of the customer.

Operational Excellence

A key component to the BOS is Operational Excellence, and how the organization will deploy its available resources to improve its overall efficiencies. The two tools most familiar to everyone when developing Operational Excellence programs are six sigma and lean manufacturing.

Six Sigma

In many organizations, six sigma, in its simplest expression, means a measure of quality that strives for near perfection. Six sigma is more than that; it is a disciplined, data-driven approach and methodology for eliminating defects (driving towards six standard deviations between the mean and the nearest specification limit) in any process, from manufacturing to transactional and from product to service.

The statistical representation of six sigma describes quantitatively how a process is performing. To achieve six sigma, a process must not produce more than 3.4 defects per million opportunities. A six sigma defect is defined as anything outside of customer specifications. A six sigma opportunity is then the total quantity of chances for a defect. Process sigma can easily be calculated using a six sigma calculator.

The fundamental objective of the six sigma methodology is the implementation of a measurement-based strategy that focuses on process improvement and variation reduction through the application of six sigma improvement projects. This is accomplished through the use of two six sigma sub-methodologies: DMAIC and DMADV. The six sigma DMAIC process (define, measure, analyze, improve and control) is an improvement system for existing processes that are falling below specification and looks for incremental improvement. The six sigma DMADV process (define, measure, analyze, design and verify) is an improvement system used to develop new processes or products at six sigma quality levels. It can also be employed if a current process requires more than just incremental improvement. Both six sigma processes are executed by six sigma green belts and six sigma black belts, and are overseen by six sigma master black belts.

According to the six sigma Academy, black belts save companies approximately $230,000 per project and can complete four to six projects per year. General Electric, one of the most successful American companies implementing six sigma, has estimated benefits on the order of $10 billion during the first 5 years of implementation. GE first began utilizing six sigma in 1995 after Motorola and Allied Signal blazed the six sigma trail. Since then, thousands of companies around the world have discovered the far reaching benefits of six sigma.[i] A list of acronyms used in six sigma is presented in the Appendix.

Lean manufacturing is a generic process management philosophy derived primarily from the Toyota Production System (TPS), but it also has origins from other sources. It is renowned for its focus on the reduction of the original Toyota-defined "seven wastes" in order to improve overall customer value.

As process tools, six sigma and lean have different functions within an organization and most companies look to some combination of both within their Operational Excellence programs. Organizations generally look to utilize lean to handle the biggest change and elimination of waste within the organization and for six sigma to handle the more focused variations in process. I have led organizations, mentored belts, and taught curriculums for both. I have been certified and familiar with both of the programs as continuous improvement tools. I believe that both the tools are important to organizations. However, because of the conditions, many organizations would prefer to focus on the lean tools. I believe that they are a little less complex in scope and can get an organization motivated if processes are implemented properly and very quickly. Creating repeatable processes and eliminating waste is something that everyone in the workplace can focus on and begin working on immediately.

Toyota Production System or Lean
The Toyota 'Just In Time' (JIT) production system, commonly known as Lean Manufacturing, was largely created by Taiichi Ohno soon after World War II. It was created out of need; necessity being the mother of invention. It did not begin to attract attention of the Japanese industry until 1973, during the first oil crisis when Japanese managers who were accustomed to inflation and a high growth rates were suddenly confronted with zero growth and forced to handle production decreases. It was during this first economic emergency that they first noticed the results Toyota was achieving with its relentless pursuit of waste elimination. They began to introduce the system into their own workplaces.[ii]

Toyota has been on its journey with the TPS for over 40 years and understands they still have a long way to go. Taiichi Ohno, in a brilliant but simple manner, explains that at Toyota "they look at a timeline. This timeline begins when they get an order to the time they collect the cash for a finished product or service. They look to reduce this timeline by removing non-value-added wastes."[iii]

As we explored the fact that many companies continue to leave the United States, we concluded that ineffective leadership and poor processes are major contributors to this phenomena. Just like the need for Toyota to develop a system geared to eliminate waste during the first oil crisis of 1973, we are in a similar situation of operating on a burning platform. Today, as we face another oil crisis and a poor economy compounded by ineffective leadership and poor processes, we must act in a similar manner. We cannot afford to look for Silver Bullets and must learn from Toyota's successes. We will not be able to carry large amounts of inventory, have processes that are not repeatable, and yield a tremendous amount of waste. We will need leaders that ensure that there is a clearly communicated vision/mission, a deployable strategy with a business operating system that ensures repeatable processes for all that is done throughout the organization. As companies begin this journey, the After Action Review process we will discuss later in this section, will provide an opportunity to reflect and learn. In this part of the book we will explore a change in culture utilizing lean processes and tools as a way of doing business that will give all businesses a better chance for success. For this part of the discussion we will need to look at the following definitions:

1. **Process** – well-defined sequence of activities that yield a desired result of an acceptable level of performance.
2. **Competency** - an organizational capability to improve a business process to a higher level of performance or desired result to gain a competitive advantage. (We will be trying to develop competencies in all employees.)
3. **Mess** - everything else.

Holistic Quality, the Company Culture and the Focus of the Customer

Establishing a culture for change is often one of the greatest challenges for companies. The principals guiding the company culture should be defined as part of the vision and mission of the company, and as you begin to establish how your culture will function, this will become a part of the strategy and, more importantly, the BOS. The culture will be defined by the customers, leadership and the employees and how they interact and function in support of the vision. The product or service the business provides will be a part of this culture as well. In a lean driven company, the focus is on people. All work processes must be controlled scientific experiments constantly modified and improved by the people who do the work. People have to be the focus as they are the greatest asset a company has, and those companies that understand this will have the greatest competitive advantage. In a lean-oriented company, the journey of continuous improvement is ongoing. The lean journey looks at how things are currently functioning and whether there is additional non value added activities occurring in any process where waste could be eliminated. There are many companies that have quality "programs" that focus on improving quality. These programs, such as TQM, ISO and others, are geared toward certification of how the company's processes are documented. This certification is intended to ensure that the company has documented its processes and that the people are following these processes in every manner. I have experienced situations where this becomes an activity to ensure there is written documentation for each process instead of being a means to achieve better quality. This certification process is normally paid for, and does focus on whether a process is documented, but it does not always ensure that the processes are improving the product or service or meeting the customer's expectations. At Toyota, or in a lean environment, quality is not perceived as a program but as a result. The way in which a company operates its processes is called "Holistic Quality." This holistic quality process places emphasis on the three basic elements of customer needs or, in fact, the Customer's Expectations. The three elements are:

1.   The timely delivery of product (per TAKT time).
2.   The cost to manufacture product (per targeted costing).
3.   The fit and function of product (per customer expectations).

Quality should not be thought of as an inspection process that is added to ensure good parts. It is not based solely on the performance, features or characteristics of a product. Quality is about people, not parts or machinery. People make decisions based on experience, tribal knowledge or personal feelings. Experiences are valuable, but two people will have different types of experience or knowledge, which can be a benefit to an organization. However, because of the variation in how it is applied, it can often be detrimental. Quality is also not a department, it is an attitude and a culture. In this type of environment where quality is cultural, the people within the organization focus on six broad areas:

1. Lean design/lean manufacturing of product.
2. Leadership by proactive participation management throughout the leadership continuum.
3. Repeatable manufacturing processes.
4. Employee empowerment.
5. Global vendor partnerships in the supply chain.
6. Quantifiable metrics (what gets measured gets fixed).

This is a cultural shift from many traditional manufacturing companies. It is a different philosophy, and a different way of conducting business. The following three elements will be measured by measurable metrics and any process found to be in noncompliance will be dealt with in an expeditious manner to achieve total customer satisfaction. At Toyota the definition of "holistic quality" is the conformance to a set of requirements. These requirements are in fact the customer expectations. Customer expectations are:

1. **Timely delivery** - How the product flows through the production area, including all production lines and work cells must be defined by the customer. The production rate should not be constrained by the varying paces of the production members, but rather by the rate the customer is consuming the product. No part of the process link can deviate from this rhythm. All non value activities that occur during the production process should be eliminated.
2. **Cost of product** - Usage of raw materials, scrap rates, yields, engineered scrap and ordering the correct parts all play a factor in the product cost. Staffing of lines in support of TAKT time is essential. How the lines or modular cells are set up. Are they based on flexibility in nature and for flow rather than function?
3. **Perceived quality** (fit & finish) and performance of product - All processes in the system must be robust and repeatable. They should be designed to handle multiple products and with quality built in rather than inspecting for it on the manufacturing floor.

Each of these expectations impacts everything that is done in manufacturing, and measures should be put in place to ensure success. Although much of the focus here is on manufacturing, all support functions should be focused in the same manner.

The internal customers should have similar metrics or requirements as the external customers.

1.   Timely delivery (change to TAKT time).
2.   Cost of product (staffing needs based on TAKT time and customer requirements).
3.   Repeatable processes documented and understood.

Each of these will be addressed in the discussion of how we manage our processes. If you do not fulfill the internal customer's requirements (expectations), you cannot fulfill the external customer's requirements. This is a very important consideration because with the poor efficiency levels of many of our faltering companies today, the focus is on the external customer and the internal processes and customers are suffering from poor performance.

As part of the company culture, it is very important to ensure that every person and every function is focused on Holistic Quality. All metrics for every function should be created utilizing the internal and external requirements of the customer. Before any quality issue can be addressed the TAKT time must be understood in its entirety because it is this TAKT time that drives everything going forward within an organization. Very simply, TAKT time is the rate at which we are selling the product, or the rate at which the customer is standing at the door waiting to pick up his/her product or service that will be delivered. This means that all processes are driven by this rate. The formula for TAKT time is: determine Real Available Minutes (RAM) in a shift and divide by the number of products (sold units). In a traditional manufacturing company, we are not producing product to fill a customers' need, but at a pace that we have normally determined by historical review and past performance. Since under this type of system we cannot react to fluctuations in demand, we build to fill a warehouse and then pay people money to manage it. We build for "just in case" and watch the inventory and company expenses add up.

The RAM is not taken into consideration. Without "real minutes" you cannot determine your capacity per shift. It is the non value added activities that impact manufacturing efficiencies. This all leads to an inability to react to production fluctuations. The greatest competitive advantage in having a TAKT time is that it affords the ability to do the following:

1. Compete in a marketplace where the demand and cost of product is being dictated by the customer.
2. Ability to pull the product down the line versus push.
3. Monitor the production rate at intervals that are much smaller than the TAKT time. When issues are found anywhere in the process that stop the series of work steps or interferes with the work being completed on time, they can be dealt with in a concise documented manner.
4. Build without overtime.
5. Determine the correct number of production workers required.
6. Affords targeted costing for labor and product.
7. Control costs more effectively.

As we begin to look at a variety of lean techniques and tools that can be helpful to any business, it will be very important to understand the following:

1. The strategic level of leadership must lead the transformation. They must lead by example. They must lead by frequent and meaningful communication, by consistent metrics; and they must lead at the front line level with active involvement. Leadership throughout the continuum must lead by example and get all employees throughout the company to actively be involved with the change. The revenues will increase dramatically with the involvement of the people, as will the collective ideas to reduce waste and create process innovation. With the leadership involved in the transformation process, it will convey the intentions of the change with active conviction.

2.   The transformation process must be included in the strategy and the BOS with clarity and support. There should be a champion assigned that is an active member of the strategic leadership team and reports primarily to the most senior leader. The support must include resources, financing, and availability of time. There are many transformation processes that are not succeeding today because of the lack of involvement of the strategic leadership team. Also, without a holistic strategy or proper resources, the change process is perceived as a "flavor of the day" window dressing, another Silver Bullet. This change must be a part of the business with deliverables and focus just as any other part of the business would be.

3.   Establish a team of people dedicated to leading the transformation. The people should have some leadership experience, process competencies and an understanding of the company vision, mission and strategy. This should include representation from the tactical level employees.

4.   Begin with a specific project that will include the current state of the process. Ensure that the project has some key objectives and deliverables that can and will be measured. Use the After Action Review process to learn from the project prior to further involvement throughout the organization.

After the above support and steps are implemented, a foundation for meaningful change will be in place. This transformation must be viewed as investment or as a necessity by the senior leadership. There have been a number of ways that organizations have deployed the lean tools, and as you know there are not many that have had holistic successes. Toyota, Harley Davidson, Dell, Boeing, Danaher and Porsche are some companies that have had relative success utilizing lean. Taiichi Ohno says: "making a factory operate for the company just like the human body operates for an individual. The autonomic nervous system responds even when we are asleep. The human body functions in good health when it is properly cared for, fed and watered correctly, exercised frequently, and treated with respect. It is only when a problem arises that we become conscious of our bodies. Then we respond by making corrections. The same thing happens in a factory. We should have a system in a factory that automatically responds when problems occur."[iv] This analogy by Mr. Ohno makes this process appear like organized common sense. We will review the steps required to look at an existing organization or planning on a new one so that it responds in this manner.

The first step will be to understand how we will organize the workplace. This will be called the "5S Program," and it is a way to introduce discipline into the workplace. Although it is often associated with housekeeping, it is in fact the start of the psychology of setting the behaviors within the workplace. The 5S's are:

1. Seiri (arrangement) - identify and segregate what belongs in an area and what does not.
2. Seiton (tidiness) - Arrange items in the area and discard those that do not belong.
3. Seiso (cleaning) - Clean daily.
4. Seiketsu (cleanliness) - Revisit frequently either daily or weekly.
5. Shitsuke (training) - Motivate to sustain.

Late delivery and defective goods often happen when the 5S has not been realized. In such places, worker morale is often low and there is very little engagement and few ideas are being exchanged. The English translation for 5s is:

1. Sort
2. Shine
3. Set in order
4. Standardize
5. Sustain

I, as well as many organizations, have included Safety as the 6th S. I have launched many 6S programs and have included the transactional areas; this is not just a manufacturing exercise. This can be used as a friendly competition between areas and functions because it has a measurable tool available to track progress. This can be one of the first true opportunities for a change environment to involve every employee in an active event, such as having a place for everything and putting everything in its place to establish discipline and order in the workplace.

The next step in the process I would recommend is called the "lean DMAIC process." It is a defined method of waste elimination for any organization and will help with problem solving. DMAIC stands for:

1. Define (D) - Define the process cycle time, lead time or TAKT time.
2. Measure (M) - Measure or map the current state processes from the start to end points. This can be done utilizing a value stream map or, in some cases, a process map that focuses primarily on a specific area.
3. Analyze (A) – Analyze value and non value added processes, constraints and process efficiencies.
4. Improve (I) - Improve to future state flow with cellular manufacturing, leveled scheduling processes, single piece flow, quick setup and cross training or other lean tools.
5. Control (C) - Control inventory and cycle time with kanban pull, visual management, mistake proofing, process FEMAs, and standard work.
6. Leverage (L) - Although this is not a constant in the DMAIC process, it is used to look at how to leverage assets and improvements made to the process within the rest of the value stream or organization.

As a separate note, the six sigma tools that use DMAIC, as well as DMAIC itself, focus on problem-solving instead of just on the process. After the DMAIC process is taught, as a defined method of waste elimination, the focus should shift to how the plant is organized. Much of this process will work in the support areas, transactional areas, and in companies outside of the manufacturing arena. There may be some modifications as to how this process works outside of manufacturing, but this should be a focus of the leadership's creativity.

Training the organization on "small lot size production" or service as needed is a key tool to focus on here. This will ensure that what is being produced will be absorbed by the customer within the given TAKT times throughout the process. It is important to ensure the waste of overproduction is eliminated whenever possible. The methods in which the work area is set up and changeovers are handled are important here. Ensuring quick changeovers for machinery or processes is important because of the time measured in seconds that it takes to stop one product being produced to another can have significant impact on process efficiencies and not keeping the customer waiting. Production should be smoothed by producing products and services in response to sales velocity.

Standard Work

Standardizing operations should be the next useful set of tools in the existing business transformation or the new business start up. Standardizing the way work is completed within the process and how workers complete their tasks are also critical in reducing variability in the process and, hence, results. The three elements of standard work are TAKT Time/Cycle Time, Work Sequence, and Standard Work in Process. It is important that each of these elements is documented and posted in the cell or work area. This three-element process depicts the flow of work in a work area and the sequence that the tasks should be performed. It will indicate the relationship of operator steps and machine cycles. Waste is readily available and is most visible when the three elements are not followed. Standard work is an excellent training tool and should be embraced by the training team that may be housed in human resources. In environments where engineering is present, it is important that the standard work be a part of the developmental process when the products are designed. This ensures involvement by the direct employees and keeps the engineering team involved in how the product will be produced. This can ultimately help with the development of repeatable processes and with the fit and form of the product.

Setting up a pull system within the workplace is the next step that will help support the TAKT times in support of your customers. This system, often referred to as "Kanban," is a total phi-

losophy of how the product will flow through a system, is purchased, and then delivered to the stations in need of performing the
next operation. Kanbans are instructions captured on documents
that, at a glance, communicate information needed at the work station. This is also a change in scope within many organizations
because it helps them to be more precise in what raw materials need
to be ordered and when. It will eliminate the guessing game cus-
tomarily used in many supply chain systems where ordering is
based on history or 'just in case.' Reducing the inventory while utilizing the Kanban system can reduce the amount of money tied up
in inventory. It will also ensure product is produced based on TAKT
times and in support of your customers needs. This also enables a
defect to be identified and fixed at the source before a significant
amount of defective product is produced.

Visual Management

The next tool that we will explore is visual management. This
is not complicated; however, it is important to have some form of
metrics in place and ensure alignment with vision, mission and strategy. It is important to have areas of your organization designated for
display of information. This information should have a standardized
key metrics area and also allow for other information about the
process or function that the information supports. This will help with
training and ensure that the common goals are supported throughout
the organization.

In brief, the introductory steps to instituting change consist of
making a schedule, setting a goal, providing educational activities,
and moving from a down-stream process to an up- stream process. It
then continues with the 5S concept and proceeds to the changing of
the layout of the facility, standard work, visual management, and
product flow based on the customer. The above tools are some examples that can be useful in helping existing organizations or start ups
to be successful from a process perspective.

There are a number of assessment tools such as lean assessments, six sigma assessments, and others available that will help you
to understand how your organization is progressing through its
process journey utilizing lean tools. Some of these tools have been

developed by companies and others by individuals. I have used a variety of these assessments to help identify the status of lean and or six sigma tools utilized in companies. These assessments have provided information that has helped me identify the current state of lean and six sigma tools and performance gaps for companies and plants worldwide.

Some of the lean tools I have used with great success are:

Lean Tools
- 5S
- Lean Kaizen DMAIC
- Continuous Flow and Pull Systems
- Standard Work
- Quick Changeover
- Total Productive Maintenance (TPM)
- Kan Ban
- Process Mapping
- TAKT and Cycle Time Analysis
- Visual Workplace
- Value Analysis/Value Engineering

Lean Activities
- Lean Simulations
- Waste Walk
- Value Stream Mapping
- Kaizen Events
- Lean Assessments

The operational excellence tools of the BOS are very important in supporting the strategy because they help to define how tasks and activities will function as a process. It is important to remember that a BOS and the tools that support it are a journey, that it is evolutionary, and can take many years to obtain all of the results possible within an organization.

AFTER ACTION REVIEW

As many organizations face the need for change in a global economy, one of the greatest competitive advantages for any business will be having an organization committed to the concept of continuous learning during growth. Learning organizations will undertake their journeys and will always evolve and change as the need occurs. This learning concept should be a part of the strategy and be of supreme importance to all leaders. In a lean-led environment, learning is part of the process and as improvement occurs, so too must the learning. The learning should be documented in some manner and involve the entire organization. I have used and continue to use The After Action Review (AAR) as a learning process.

The AAR is a technique that was originated by the US Army to improve team performance by analyzing the actions taken and the results for any given unit. I have been able to translate much of its value into the business world for a few companies I have worked. "For America's Army, the AAR was the key to turning the corner and institutionalizing organizational learning. You will probably never become a learning organization in any absolute sense; it can only be something you aspire to, always becoming but never truly being. But, in the Army, the AAR has ingrained a respect for organizational learning, fostering an expectation that decisions and consequent actions will be reviewed in a way that will benefit both the participants and the organization; no matter how painful it may be at the time. The only real failure is the failure to learn." General Gordon Sullivan, US Army (retired) (taken from the book "HOPE is NOT A METHOD"; New York; Broadway Books; p 193, by Gordon Sullivan and Michael Harper).

The AAR is considered to be a very valuable and useful tool. Many believe that it is "arguably the major single influence on the revolution in training that took place in the US Army in the more than twenty years following the end of the Vietnam War." (Anne Chapman, "The National Training Center Matures, 1985-1993," TRADOC Historical Monograph.) The utilization of AARs in business situations hold the promise of providing a straightforward way to improve performance and generate knowledge in dealing with virtually any challenge or opportunity in virtually any group or situation, and is a great tool for support to the strategy or BOS.

The AAR process allows organizations to learn both what works and what does not, from prior actions, and can be a tool that helps foster a learning culture within an organization. In many of today's companies there are decisions being made by people in leadership roles that are causing the failure of their businesses, and for many Americans, a loss of jobs. In addition to these failed decisions, many organizations do not have a structured process in which to learn by these failures. The AAR is a tool that will provide leaders data for analyzing and supporting many decisions involving projects, programs, and actions within the organization, and allow for realignment of priorities when unintended consequences are detected. An additional benefit of this tool is the amount of employee involvement opportunities available to companies that will add significant value to a process, project or program during the early stages of development. This will enable an organization to maximize the effectiveness of the change and will have the added ability to foster buy-in and support of its employees.

I had the opportunity to learn the AAR process during my time as an officer in the US Army. As I transitioned to the corporate world, I realized its applicability of the process and began to utilize it to assist me in many of my roles. Early on, I was able to use the AAR as a feedback process to share information with my teams and provide definable documentation to my superiors. When I joined Harley Davidson, I was able to implement an AAR process for my teams in manufacturing and to greatly increase the efficiency of the processes and the speed at which change was affected.

As Director of Manufacturing at Harley Davidson, I was able to utilize this process during the manufacturing launch for the VRod motorcycle and the new Sportster. This was the first new vehicle family launched at Harley Davidson in over 50 years, so there was a serious lack of experience for this type activity. A challenging part of this new vehicle launch was that the launch was happening in one of Harley Davidson's newest facilities, which was set up utilizing a nontraditional type of operating structure. The operating structure consisted of a decision-making process that involved requiring an almost 100% consensus in decision-making between the salaried and hourly employees. Although the involvement with all employees was a benefit and great in concept, this presented some serious hurdles. Being a new plant, the experience levels or technical process skills were not equivalent to those present at other facilities around the company. The challenge was that some of the changes were not understood and this affected the pace of the decision-making process. These technical shortcomings also manifested themselves in the execution effectiveness required for new product and process development.

My intent for utilizing the AAR process was to implement a learning tool that would help establish clear expectations for a project or program, and the representative employees of every function, throughout a phase gate methodology while fostering a tremendous amount of involvement and feedback while learning. This also allowed for necessary changes throughout the processes and the predictability of the end state. The AAR process can be used at any time within any function of any organization where change is needed or continuous improvement and learning is desired.

With our focus on safety of the employees, cost, quality, and delivery of the product, we were able to understand what a realistic expectation for the customer would be. This expectation engendered a better understanding of the cost to manufacture, what quality levels could be expected, and how long it would actually take to go through the manufacturing operations. This process involved every functional area of the value stream involved in producing the product. Engineering, Supply Chain, Operations, Finance, Human Resources, and IT, were all part of the process. Every area had common metrics that were set prior to the start of the program, and we established a set of assumptions for the program in the beginning, based on the metrics, so that we were able to focus our AAR. In the assumptions, we focused on key metrics that included: Cost, Delivery, Quality (fit and form), and a Continuous Improvement plan for each phase or build event.

Cost: Every functional area had to develop cost metrics as it pertained to that area. The costs had to be estimated with 5% expense variation and 2% capital variation. The accountability included how many people we would need and how much it would cost to train them, any overtime, and how much the prototype parts would be. We also wanted to begin to understand the TAKT time (TAKT time can be defined as the maximum time allowed to produce a product in order to meet demand). It is derived from the German word taktzeit, which translates to "clock cycle").ᵛ This was very important, because it put accountability into the process and ensured that we were not building waste into the new system.

Delivery: Every functional area had to commit to delivery times for all aspects of the build process. We did not focus just on when the sequences would be completed but on everything in the process. We were measuring delivery times of parts, new hires, drawings, station builds and overall performance to the TAKT times.

Quality; each functional area was measured on the quality of the work that they produced for each of their customers. Supply chain and engineering were held accountable for supplier quality at this point as well. As we were setting up the build stations on the new assembly line, we wanted to ensure design for manufacturability and accurate build sequences for the work instructions as we created standard work. As we began developing the quality standards required, the establishment of TAKT times for the build process was extremely helpful in establishing AAR parameters.

Continuous Improvement: As part and a result of the AAR process, I wanted to ensure that each team focused on getting better after each build event. While the assumptions in this portion of the plan focused on the improvement part, the end state would be a process that yielded a predictable product with good assumptions regarding TAKT time, delivery, quality and manufacturing cost.

As the initial assumptions were developed prior to the start of the program and after each build event, we performed a comprehensive AAR. The AAR process involved representatives from all functions that were part of the complete launch system, including hourly employees, all with the same level of input as engineering, supply chain and senior staff. As we went through the AAR process, we focused on five key areas and reviewed how each function performed based on the initial assumptions. The five key areas we used as the basis for the meeting were:

1. What went well? And why?
2. What did not go as per the assumptions/plan? And why?
3. What were the lessons learned?
4. What would that functional group do differently, if they had known what they experienced during the build event?
5. What are the next steps? (This step included the planning and assumptions for the next build event, leading to the official launch of the VROD program.)

The AAR process was handled in a manner where all employees were equal, and all input was documented. The documentation aided us as we progressed through each of the steps of the build process for this program, but it would also be a tool that was available for all subsequent progra]ms. The involvement and impact of customers being represented throughout the entire value stream allowed for people to communicate different views of the issues, problems, and concerns as they related to our defined assumptions and metrics. With the focus of the questions, as defined, learning why things went well or not as planned is the key. Even if the process went as planned in the assumptions, understanding why it did so will help to solidify the process to ensure that "luck" is not included as part of a predictable process. The AAR process was very effective in helping to experience an improved performance through each build event, increased involvement, and buy-in of employees in each area and an expansion of communication and accountability. The learning level experienced by all was tremendous. By the time the official launch of the program arrived, which we referred to as Job 1, we had made a significant amount of progress in TAKT time and the other measurable areas. The entire team experienced an enviable level of success and growth in the launch of the VROD program.

A Learning Organization
For the AAR process to be most effective as a tool for leaders, they must integrate it as a learning opportunity to positively impact the organization. It will be a chance for employees closest to a product or service to have input, and this input will become part of the holistic quality culture that is in place to meet or exceed the

customer's expectations. The AAR should be part of the strategic planning process so that it becomes part of the DNA of the organization. You can execute an AAR event after almost any activity that occurs in an organization. They can be a short impromptu lesson, or a longer more intense session for more complex situations. I am sure that as leaders we all want an organization that is continually growing; this tool can become a best friend and, if utilized properly, it can be very effective for developing a learning organization culture within your business. Below is a visual of the AAR process.

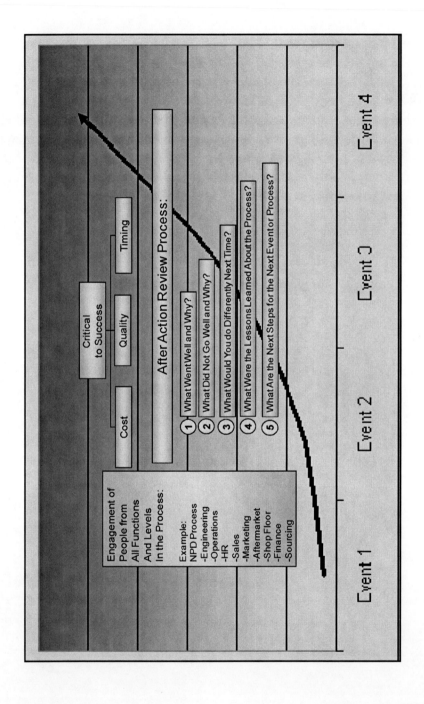

COMMUNICATIONS

In section entitled "Instituting Change," we covered some very important keys to successfully transforming an organization. We covered the Business Operating System, Operational Excellence (which included some lean and six sigma tools), and the After Action Review process. Now we will explore some of the key ingredients for linking together the above strategic tools and a business's employees. The first of the ingredients, Communication, is often discussed and frequently used as an excuse by many people at all levels of an organization when inefficiencies exist. Communication is also often used as the rationale for not knowing or not getting things done. I have heard, as I am sure that many of you have, employees at various levels of organizations say:

1. No one told me
2. I did not know anything about that
3. I did not know
4. That's not my job
5. Do you know how we are doing?
6. How did we do?
7. Did you hear the rumor ...
8. What is our goal today? This month? This year?
9. Are we doing better?
10. How does my job impact the big picture?
11. We have always done things this way

Whether it is communicating the vision, mission, or strategy throughout the organization, company performance, or an employee's understanding of how they fit into the organization, communication is critical to the success of every business. It is the responsibility of the strategic leader, as well as every leader throughout the leadership continuum, to ensure that communication is a key tool in every organization. Communication can be the glue that holds the entire organization together, or without it can tear it apart. Because of how important this is to all organizations, the communications plan should be a part of the overall strategy. That strategy must include how information will flow through the organization, how problems will be handled and solutions achieved, how company and individual metrics or performance will be discussed, how feedback mechanisms will be performed when dealing with suppliers, customers, and visitors. These are a few examples of the types of communication that may need to occur in organizations but it is clearly not all. Company meetings need to be defined with a structure. This is important because you want to ensure that the meetings are effective, concise, and clearly attain their objectives without wasting time.

Status codes are an effective way of ensuring that meetings are effective and do not waste time. This is where every functional area of an organization is given a code. During meetings all issues and bottlenecks that impact the customer are discussed by the appropriate code. The issues are addressed by the appropriate codes and these are tracked by number and frequency of occurrences so that the root causes of the problems are identified, documented and solved.

The time of all employees is valuable and cost the company when wasted. I have instituted a 1-hour time limit for meetings in some of my organizations. The intent was to ensure that the meetings started on time, everyone was prepared, and solving problems and staying focused on the objectives was the goal. Because everyone was clear about the objectives and the meeting structure and plan had been communicated, to all employees, this was not difficult. There were some times where issues and concerns had to be addressed after the meeting, but this was often planned for and discussed. I believe that in addition to establishing some discipline within the organization, it also sent a clear message that I considered everyone's time valuable and that being efficient and focusing on eliminating waste in all we do is part of the DNA or culture of the company. The important thing to remember when developing a communication plan is that it should include:

- how things will be communicated,
- how often,
- where they will be communicated and
- by whom.

During my tenure at Harley Davidson we focused a great deal on communications because the employees were valued as one of our greatest assets. There was a tremendous amount of communication we conducted because of our commitment to employee involvement and the strong relationship we had with the unions. We spent a great deal of time and invested a lot of money in meetings. As we were going through changes, we communicated with increased frequency to ensure all employees knew what was going on and how they would be able to help or if they might be impacted. We communicated to the various stakeholders daily, monthly, and quarterly. The meetings were often conducted jointly with the union, and almost always had representation from the senior leadership of the company. It did not matter what time these meetings were held, leadership was present at all meetings. There was a tremendous commitment to ensure that the organization understood how we were performing as a company and being able to address employee issues and concerns. While I believe that the attempts to ensure communications to everyone regarding the status of what was happening in the company and marketplace that Harley Davidson was operating in was effective, if it had been combined with a holistic strategy and more defined focused on the current state of the organization I am sure that the realized results would have been even more dramatic.

I have seen organizations where there was not an effective communication plan and there is always a visible disconnect within the organization and a state of constant nervousness in the employees. These organizations were invariably focused on the financials and operated in a chaotic environment of unpredictable processes that always generated unpredictable results. Some considerations for an effective communications plan are:

- consistent themes
- tailored to address stakeholder interests
- Reflect the core purpose and values of the organization, its vision and mission
- provides credibility and relevance through data
- energized by examples and data
- tailored to various forums to reach all stakeholders at all levels with relevance

- have a consistent frequency to ensure involvement, engagement and interest by all employees
- define Champions at all levels
- have a mechanism for feedback and addressing issues and concerns
- provide a method of follow-up

The frequency for communication can be considered daily, weekly, monthly, quarterly and annually. An example of a communication plan I have used is provided in the Appendix. This communication plan will help keep employees engaged and focuses on defined metrics so that all employees will be able to keep score on how well they or the organization is performing. The strategic leadership team will find that when there is an effective communication plan in place that it will be an enabler for the vision, mission and strategy.

Rewards and Recognition
All employees enjoy rewards and recognition for their hard work! Rewarding employees for their hard work is something designed to let people know that they are appreciated regardless of their role or position within the organization. The reward does not need to be expensive, but should reflect acknowledgment for the efforts by the employee, team or company based on their achieving certain goals or going beyond the normal expectations. I have used trinkets, different types of food, celebrations, cash awards, entertainment tickets, certificates and sometimes a great big public 'thank you' followed by a handshake. There should be a system established to ensure that all employees are being treated equally and favoritism does not overshadow the intent. Giving rewards can be a sensitive area because some employees do not want to be singled out for their accomplishments and some organizations, particularly union environments, do not like to have individuals rewarded. In these environments, I have used creative means to reward employees in private with small tokens of appreciation, or a hand shake and thank you. I have always tried to be consistent with my administration of rewards and recognition, and have always believed that they are an important

part of any organization. There were many times I used my own money and not company funds because I believed that the employee or team deserved special recognition. I have given awards to subordinates in the military, such as birthday cakes, that always engendered a surprising level of heartfelt emotion from the tough soldiers. During my time at Harley Davidson, the CEO sent all employees birthday cards. I always appreciated the messages I received in my cards, which highlighted some of my accomplishments. I have borrowed this tactic of giving birthday cards since leaving Harley Davidson and have experienced tremendous response from employees.

All of the positions I have had in corporate America involved change, start up, or business growth, and all of these roles were heavily dependent on the participation of the employees. Because I believe that people are the greatest asset an organization can have, the importance of rewards and recognition are paramount. It is very important in change environments where employees are learning different tasks or processes that rewards and recognition are an integral part of the plan. It is also important that the rewards and recognition are not over-used or used for performing within the normal expectations of the job. This can have the negative effect of instilling a sense of entitlement and reduce creativity within the workplace. Giving rewards or recognizing people for less than performance above expectations or for rewarding mediocre employees can cause discontent amongst your overachieving employees. There is no formula for identifying the best program; however, the focus of a rewards and recognition program must be on the employees and on continuously improving the organization. The intent of the program is to show appreciation from the company for employees that perform above expectations or go beyond the call of service for the benefit of the company. Remember that an unexpected and sincere thank you, either in public or private, can mean more to the recipient than any other type of recognition, and it can do wonders for morale.

Putting It All Together

Successful leaders challenge themselves and their organizations to thrive on change. With all of the changes that our country is going through, having the necessary skills and competencies required for being a leader is more important than ever. Becoming a successful leader will give your entire business a better sense of direction, will foster alignment of the employees (your greatest asset) across the enterprise, and will provide a foundation for long-term financial success.

Beyond just having the title of "leader," having and developing the competencies required for real leadership and fostering a system to build leaders within your organization is the first step in developing a holistic strategy for success that doesn't rely on hope. By studying and understanding your role and the roles of your subordinates in the leadership continuum, you can begin to institute a culture of change as well as provide the tools required to provide a direction for your organization that all employees can understand and support. Having an effective leader at the head with a clear vision/mission, a well thought-out strategy, and an engaged workforce will prepare any organization for maximizing its potential for both the circumstances under its control and the unexpected eventualities that will arise.

There are many responsibilities that leaders at each level should delegate, but they also need to know which ones they cannot delegate for an organization to be successful. This is where establishing a reporting structure and having metrics is so instrumental. One of the quickest ways to create more stress in a system is to start instituting change and not clearly defining the people's roles and responsibilities and having a way of measuring every process of every function within the organization.

There are other factors surrounding the long-term viability or level of success for any company, such as understanding the customer's expectations, adjustments in the product or service that you provide, and dealing with economic conditions. One of the greatest challenges today's leader faces is to understand the current state of their business. By knowing exactly where you are, you are able to set a holistic direction with accountability throughout any organization. Many organizations and companies know they are having problems, but because they have not taken the time to clearly define the current state, they are seeking Silver Bullets for success that are not targeted close enough to the actual problems to provide long-term solutions. This failure in leadership is a major contributor to the downward spiral of many failing organizations, including financial, healthcare, and educational institutions. There are many who will continue to fault the economy, global warming, the government, and other reasons they see as beyond their control when things are not going well. The truth is, although these may be contributing factors, the root cause of the issues facing many of us today is the failure of the leadership to take the time to pin point the exact problems that need fixing and the importance or criticality of each issue. Once you have developed the current state of your organization and established the initial priorities list, it is time to get serious about a plan.

To develop and implement a plan with a clear vision with an executable strategy, you as the leader need to take the bull by the horns and make some decisions. The decisions will be most effective if they are supported by data and not gut feel. I often remind many of my subordinates that "in God we trust, everyone else brings data." If you fail to define the vision/mission or are being unrealistic with the current state, you will again position yourself to be relying on hope and Silver Bullets, such as lean or six sigma, to solve the problems of your organization. Remember that developing the vision for your organization is not a democratic process, it is a leadership function. You can get input and attempt to get buy-in or foster support, but ultimately it is your job and your decision, and it must be in a form that can be readily communicated and understood by everyone in the company.

As the title of this book says, "HOPE IS NOT A STRATEGY." A strategy is a plan of action that you and your people are going to take to become a success. It does not matter whether you are involved in a new or existing venture, you must understand what your customer's expectations are, the quality they expect, and the price they are willing to pay. Every leader throughout the continuum must understand what it is that they are responsible for, and that they will be held accountable through measurable metrics. You are going to need a plan that is more than a series of pro-forma financials. By utilizing the complete holistic strategy or the 3-year strategy matrix process, your plan will be a step-by-step 'how to' guide with realistic tools for assessing progress in order to support the unbiased but cohesive vision, allowing you to anticipate every eventuality, and have you prepared to meet any challenge at a moment's notice. This does not mean that everything will be perfect or things will still not go wrong! Conditions will change, circumstances will change, but having an understanding of what it is you are responsible for and a direction with 'how to's' in the form of an execution plan will allow you to react with swiftness and cohesion that will be a huge competitive advantage. You will be able, as I have, to rely on this understanding and these basic tools through much adversity and challenges in different companies, in different industries, and different products, with a similar level of success.

Being an effective leader and having a plan will enable you to institute change and become a super efficient organization that will blow the socks off of the global competition and become the envy of the world and the darling of Wall Street. It is much nicer to be leading Wall Street or your investors than to have them dictating strategy to you. The development of a holistic strategy can take you from being a leader who reacts from gut feel or emotional ties to friends and existing relationships, to one who acts based on the use of effective process tools to get results. A leader is a person who understands how to get the right people on the team while utilizing the strengths and weaknesses of their skill sets based on needs of a clearly defined vision, and holding everyone and every function accountable through measurable metrics based on the customer needs.

Now that you understand leadership and have a solid plan that you can communicate to the entire organization, it is time to build an effective Business Operating System that supports the strategy and includes a roadmap for the implementation of an effective operational excellence program that may include lean and six sigma tools, or others. While many organizations and companies are using these tools as Silver Bullets, usually with limited success. Because of the work you have put in to accurately identify issues throughout the current state assessment, success is no longer a matter of hope, you are instituting change with a purpose. You are anticipating results based on an effective plan and a roadmap with how to's for all the processes. As icing on the cake, the After Action Review process you have prepared enables you to confirm those results and allows fine tuning of the systems for even greater success.

Finally, you have instituted a comprehensive communications program. By communicating effectively with your people, you are able to reduce the level of stress that comes when change is introduced. You are able to improve the speed at which they buy into change and thereby multiply the efficiency of the overall process.

All of the parts we have discussed are essential when instituting change and moving from hope to strategy. While you can definitely improve your odds by focusing on any one or two of the points, it is a commitment to the whole process and the whole value stream that can insure long-term success. Once you have taken the time to develop these tools, in any company regardless of industry, company or product, you will know that whatever life deals you can face it head on with a confident expectation of achieving results that others only hope for. It is CRITICAL to understand that this kind of transformation is not a short-term event, but a journey that will take lots of understanding and plenty of time and resources. It will not necessarily be easy and it will challenge your preconceptions and force you to change yourself and grow. Whether you are leading a manufacturing company, healthcare organization, the educational system or even the entertainment industry remember that it has taken Toyota over 50 years to be one of the best in the world, and Harley Davidson almost 20 years, to realize the transformation. Having effective leadership and a strong visioning and strategy process will ensure success for any company, solving the root cause issues of the plethora of problems within the DNA of their organizations. There is hope, and it has its foundation in strategy.

Appendix

SIX SIGMA ACRONYMS

AD-Axiomatic Design
ANOVA – Analysis of Variation
BB – Black Belt
BOM – Bill of Material
C&E – Cause and Effect
C/O – Change Over Time
C/T- Cycle Time
CA –Customer Attributes
CCD – Concurrent Composite Design
CE – Concurrent Engineering
CFM – Continuous Flow Manufacturing
CI – Confidence Interval
CLT – Central Limit Theorem
COGS – Cost of Goods and Services
COPQ – Cost of Product Quality
COQ – Cost of Quality
CP –Control Plan
CT – Critical to
CTC – Critical to Cost
CTD – Critical to Delivery
CTP – Critical to Process/Product/Service
CTQ – Critical to Quality
CTS – Critical to Satisfaction
CV – Coefficient of Variation
DES – Discrete Event Simulation
Det. – Detectability
DF – Degrees of Freedom
DFM/A –Design for Manufacturing/Assembly
DFMEA – Design Failure Modes and Effect Analysis
DFSS – Design for Six Sigma
DMAIC – Define Measure Analyze Improve Control
DOE – Design of Experiment
DP – Design Parameters
DPMO – Defects per Million Opportunities

DPO – Defects per Opportunity
DPU – Defect(s) per Unit
E&S – Evaluate and Synthesize
E/Q*A – Effectiveness is a Function of Acceptance
EH&S – Employee Health and Safety
FG – Finished Goods
FIFO – First In First Out
FMEA – Failure Modes and Effect Analysis
FOV – Families of Variation
FR – Functional Requirements
FTE- Full Time Equivalent
GB – Green Belt
HOQ – House of Quality
IDOV – Identify Design Optimize Validate
IFR – Ideal Final Result
IFR –Ideal Final Result
IPO – Input Process Output
JIT – Just in Time
KIS – Keep It Simple
KPIV – Key Process Input Variable
KPOV – Key Process Output Variable
L/T – Lead Time
LCL – Lower Control Limit
LIFO – Last In First Out
LSL – Lower Specification Level
LT - Long Term
M (4 M's) - Manpower, Machinery, Materials, Measurements
MBB – Master Black Belt
MGP – Multi-Generation Planning
MRP – Materials Requirement Planning
MS – Mean Square
MSA – Measurement System Error
MSE – Mean Square Error
MTBF - Mean Time Between Failure
NOP – Net Operating Profit
NP&SI – New Product and Service Introduction
NVA – Non- Value Added

NVAN – Non-Value Added but Necessary
Occ. – Occurrence
OFAT – One Factor At a Time
PDCA – Plan Do Check Act
PERMIA - Performance Measures Independent of Adjustment
PFMEA – Process/Product Failure Mode Effective Analyses
PIV – Process Input Variable
PM –Preventative Maintenance
POV- Process output Variable
PPM –Parts per Million
PV - Process Variables
QFD – Quality Function Diagram
QFD – Quality Function Deployment
R&R – Repeatability and Reproducibility
ROIC – Return on Investment Capital
RPD - Robust Parameter Design
RPN – Risk Priority Number
RRA – Risk Response Actions
RRS – Risk Response Strategies
RSM – Response Surface Methodology
RTY – Rolled Throughput Yield
S.W.O.T - Strength Weaknesses Opportunities Threats
SD – Standard Deviation
SE – Standard Error
SEM – Standard Error of the Mean
Sev. – Severity
SIPOC – Supplier Input Process Output Customer
SMART – Specific Measurable Attainable Relevant Timely
SMED – Single Minute Exchange of Dyes
SN Ratio –Signal to Noise Ratio
SOP – Standard Operating Procedure
SPC – Statistical Process Control
SS –Sum of Squares
ST - Short Term
STE Design – Special Test Equipment Design
TAP – Transformation Acceleration Process
TAPs – Target Adjusting Parameters

TD – Tolerance Design
TDU – Total Defects per Unit
TOP – Total number of Opportunities
TPM - Total Productive Maintenance
TPY – Throughput Yield
TRIZ –Theory of Inventive Problem Solving
UCL – Upper Control Limit
USL – Upper Specification Limit
VA – Value Added
VA/T – Value Added Time
VAPs – Variation Adjusting Parameters
VIP - Variation Inducing Parameters
VOC – Voice of the Customer
VOP – Voice of the Process
VSM – Value Stream Map
W/T – Work Time
WBS – Work Breakdown Structure
WIP – Work in Process
Y_{final} – Final Yield
Y_{norm} – Normalized Yield
Y_{rt} – Rolled Throughput Yield
Y_{tp} – Throughput Yield

Lean Enterprise

5 Principles of Lean:

1. Specify value in the eyes of the customer.
2. Identify the value stream and eliminate waste.
3. Make value flow at the "pull" of the customer.
4. Involve and empower employees.
5. Continuously improve in pursuit of perfection.

Value-Added: An activity that changes the size, shape, fit, form, or function of material or information (for the first time) to meet customer requirements. The customer is willing to pay for it.
Non-Valued-Added: Activities that take time and resources but do not add to customer requirements.

Seven Types of Waste:
-Defeats-do not meet customer requirements or create rework
-Over Production-made too much and not used or sold.
-Transportation-excess distance traveled.
-Waiting-idle time of operator or goods waiting until the next step.
-Inventory-excess amount purchased and waiting to be used.
-Motion-excess movement of operator and/or part.
-Processing-unnecessary or repeated steps performed.
-THE EIGHTH TYPE OF WASTE IS PEOPLE

Lean Definitions or Acronyms

Baseline Analysis: A process which creates understanding of an opportunity, determines where to start, shapes a vision and documents an improvement plan.

Value Stream: All the actions (both value added and non-valued added) currently required to bring a product or service through the main flows essential to every product or service.

Takt Time: The "beat" of production or customer demand stated in time

Lead Time: The total elapsed time from when a customer places an order to the time when the customer receives the order.

Throughput Time: The total amount of time for a process to complete one product or service.

Cycle Time: The total amount of clock time required to complete one part including walking, load/unload, inspect and return to start.

Bottleneck or Constraint: Any area, workstation, or process that limits throughput; any problem area that slows down the whole.

Standard Work: Defines the amount of work content performed by each operator in order to achieve a balanced flow and linear output rate. A breakdown of work into elements and used to balance work content in a flow process in order to achieve a particular daily rate ideally equal to customer demand.

Kanban: A Japanese word that means "signboard". A signal authorizing production or delivery of required material and is initiated by consumption.

Service Policy: A management decision about the acceptable level of response to customer demand. The "service level" describes the likelihood that the producer will supply the customer s specific product on a specific date.

Setup Reduction: An operating technique that systematically reduces and eliminates the time and skill to set-up a piece of operating equipment or process in order to produce small quantities of high quality output at an economical cost.

Setup Time: The amount of clock time taken to change over a piece of equipment from the end of the last piece of a production lot to the first piece of the next production lot.

Internal Setup Time: Time in which the machine must be stopped to perform.

External Setup Time: Time which can be done off line while the machine is running.

SMED: Single Minute Exchange of Die- Changeover is accomplished in less than 10 minutes.

I-C-E Methodology: Identify, convert and eliminate steps during setup reduction.

Visual Controls: Creating standards in the workplace that make it obvious if anything is out of order so every employee can see it and take appropriate action.

Visual Management: System enabling anyone to quickly spot abnormalities in the workplace, regardless of their knowledge of the process.

Autonomation: The concept of adding an element of human judgment to automated equipment so that the equipment becomes capable of discriminating against unacceptable quality and the automated process becomes more reliable. A contraction of "autonomous automation."

ADD: Average Daily Demand.

R: Replenishment Time.

OEE: Overall Equipment Effectiveness.

UDE: Undesirable effect.

UDO: Undesirable observation

Lean Methodologies

Total Production Maintenance: A methodology to progress from unscheduled maintenance to scheduled maintenance to maintain flow in a flow process highly dependent on automatic machines. Needs to be addressed in the final design of a machining flow process.

5S: Methodology for creating and maintaining a clean, organized and high performing workplace. Results in safer working conditions and greater productivity/efficiency. Useful all the time whether to introduce a continuous improvement culture or included in the final design of a lean cell or line.

- **Sorting**-get rid of what is not needed
- **Storage**-organized what is left, arrange and identify for ease of use.
- **Shining**-clean up what is left. Clean daily with visual sweeps.
- **Standardizing**-make all area function the same way. Integrate sort, storage and shine into regular work activities with maintenance and check points put in place.
- **Sustaining**-set discipline following the rules, develop a schedule and stick to it, assign responsibilities.

Lean Tools

Value Stream Map: A mapping tool to show the interaction of information flow with product/material flow to identify leverage points. Used as project selection tool especially when determining potential bottlenecks and lack of linkage between processes and/or functions.

Activity of the Product or Product Process Flow (PPF): A tool utilizing a standard Lean form that identifies the amount of time the product spends in one of four conditions: Storage, Transportation, Inspection and Processing. It is useful when completing a cell baseline when you want to "staple yourself to an order/product".

Process Flow Map: A mapping tool to show visually how a process or product flows. Used to show the output after completing Activity of the Product form to capture the current and future process.

Spaghetti Chart: A visual tool to show the amount of distance traveled during a process. Usually completed during a cell baseline, it is a good tool to visually communicate to management how much non-value added travel occurs during a process.

Timed Value Map: A tool to visually display the percentage of time a product or service spends in value added or non-value added activities, or in queue (waiting). Usually completed during site or cell baseline, it is another good tool to visually communicate to management how much non- value added and queue time occurs during a process.

Activity of the Operator or Operator Observation: A tool used to capture operator activities and times utilizing a standard Lean form. Used during the beginning of a lean project to capture operator cycle times as an input into the current load chart.

Operator or Assembly Analysis: An analysis tool to identify whether operator activities and movements are VA/NVA. Used after completion of the Activity of the Operator form and videotape to analyze what can be eliminated, improved etc...

Activity of the Machine or Machine Observation: A tool used to capture various activities around the machine (set-up, load, run) utilizing a standard Lean form and videotaping. Used during a Lean project that is highly dependent on machine utilization.

Machine Analysis: A tool used to identify activities around the machine that need to be eliminated, improved (reduced) in order to meet takt time. Used after completion of Activity of the Machine to capture improvement ideas and current capacity.

Process Capacity Table: A tool used to determine how many products you can make within a flow machining process when compared to takt time. Used in a Lean project during machine analysis.

Muti-Cycle Analysis: A tool used to investigate a particular process step that shows a lot variation. Used after Activity of the Operator only on steps that show too much variation and an average estimate does not capture the true picture. Good demonstrate facts behind the estimates

Load Chart: A tool to visually show if a particular operator or machine has too much or too little work compared to takt time. Helpful in identifying where to work in order to balance the line.

Product Process Matrix or Part Family Rationalization: A tool used to determine product families and to determine potential standard routing/flow opportunities. Used in the early stages of a Lean or transition project to determine appropriate cells to create in order to maximize flow opportunities.

Group Technology or Product-Process Cycle Time Chart: A tool used to group products into families of similar cycle times. Used during the initial phrases of a site or product line's Lean journey to establish flow loops.

Organizational Alignment Chart: A visual tool that creates a picture of the integration (or lack thereof) between functional areas. Used during a site or product line baseline to show management how spread out operations is and how dependent they are on other support functions.

Area Map/Layout: Used to give an overall picture of the affected area during a baseline. Good way to show lean launch areas and to highlight shared areas between department/cells.

Inventory Location Diagram: A visual tool that provides a snapshot of actual inventory levels on hand and square footage required to store the material during a baseline. A way to capture waste in inventory and storage area and to capture potential cash flow savings. Includes raw material, WP and final goods inventory.

Monument Strategy: A tool to determine how you want to attack internal and external monuments/shared resources during your Lean project. Useful during the initial stages of a site/cell baseline to document decisions around shared resources and as an input into the capital plan.

Block Layout: A tool used to sketch a layout concept which will serve as the basis for the "To Be" process. Useful during a site or product line baseline to allocate space and to position shared resources.

Cause and Effect Matrix: A tool used to link effects to cause in order to eliminate the root cause of problems. Used during a baseline in order to identify the few causes that lead to many undesirable effects (UDEs). Effective after completion of a Value Stream Map.

Ergonomic Risk Checklist: Used to evaluate the various types of health, safety (ergonomic) and environmental risks associated with a process. Used during a lean project to evaluate the current process as well as the "To-Be" design.

Set-up Reduction (S/U Time Observation): A tool used to identify setup steps and to classify steps as either internal or external utilizing the I-C-E methodology. Used after Activity of the Machine to reduce setup times and eventually lot or batch size.

Failure Mode and Effects Analysis (FMEA): A systematic technique to identify potential failures modes, prioritize the failure modes according to risk and to identify actions which can reduce/eliminate failure modes. Used during a Lean project on both the "As-Is" and "To-Be" processes/designs.

Improvement Documentation Sheet: A form to capture and document improvement ideas that will support the final or "To-Be" design/processes.

Standard Work Sheet: A visual control tool to help the operator, supervisor and manager maintain Standard Work including standard work combinations and SWIP levels.

Standard Work Combination Sheet (SWCS): A tool/form to document the interaction between operators and machines. The first step in determining standard operation routine that can be accomplished within takt time. Also a good visual control tool.

Demand Segmentation (Cv Analysis): A tool to determine potential cells or dedicated focused factories based on volume and variability. Used during a site baseline in conjunction with Group Technology.

Demand Segmentation (Cv Analysis) for Material Ordering Policy: A tool used to determine your material ordering policy (rate-based, Kanban or MRP push) again based on volume and variability. Used during cell/line design to link up ordering policy with execution.

Changeover Matrix: A tool used to highlight significant changeover time variation based on part number or tool combinations. Used during cell/line design as an input into mixed-model sequencing.

Level-Loading or Load Smoothing: A tool to smooth demand variation to balance and synchronize operations. Used with or without Heijunka for a fixed repeating schedule during line design to mitigate demand variation.

Heijunka: A tool used to buffer demand variation in order to run a fixed repeating schedule. Used during line design in order to determine a way to perform production scheduling around internal or external monuments.

Mixed-Model Sequencing: A tool to manage the demand in mixed model cell in order to determine the best sequence of models/P/Ns. Used during line design of mixed model cell or shared resource.

PQ Analysis: A tool to determine the part numbers for mixed model cells. Similar to demand segmentation to determine dedicated verse mixed models cells. Used during a site or cell baseline.

Standard WIP (SWP): A tool used to determine the amount of WIP needed to maintain the flow especially in man-machine operations. Used during line design and shows up on the Standard Work Sheet.

Strategic Inventory-Replenishment Buffer: A tool or calculation to determine the amount of inventory at the end of a line to respond to instantaneous demand for a different product due to problems with changeovers. Used during line deign. Also, see Product Family Turnover Ratio.

Product Family Turnover Ratio: A tool or calculation to determine the replenishment buffer size needed because of run times, number of models and changeover times. Useful during the design of a mixed model cell

Strategic Inventory-Service Buffer: A tool or calculation to determine the amount of inventory needed to absorb the variation or to deal with inflexible capacity. Used during cell or line design in conjunction with Heijunka

In-Process Kanban (IPK): A tool to pace the movement of products visually in a flow process (flow control). Used during line design of a flow process to determine when to work and when not to work.

Material/Supplier Kanban: A visual execution tool to authorize the production or replenishment of material when consumed from the strategic inventory buffer. Used during line design to link the planning/ordering policy to execution. Need to determine if it is best for one-card specific, two-card specific or one-card generic.

Production Control or Scheduling Board: A visual control tool to display where units are and to indentify problems or bottleneck areas/steps. Incorporated into a lean final design as part of the management control plan.

Lean Formulas or Calculations

Takt Time = $\dfrac{\text{Time Available}}{\text{Average Demand}}$

Staffing Requirements = $\dfrac{\text{Total Labor Cycle Time}}{\text{Takt Time}}$

Inventory Turnover = $\dfrac{\text{Annual \$ Sales at Cost}}{\text{Average \$ Inventory}}$

Inventory Turnover = $\dfrac{\text{Last Month's Issues x 12}}{\text{Current or Month End Inventory}}$
(For RM and WP)

Amount of Standard WIP	Manual	Automatic
-Same Direction	0	1
-Opposite Direction	1	2

Kanban Lot Size = ADD x R + (1 + safety factor)

Kanban Lot Size = (ADD x R) + (service factor x std dev)

Of Kanbans = $\dfrac{\text{ADD x R x (1 + safety factor)}}{\text{Standard container quantity}}$

Safety Factor = (Highest Demand – ADD)/ADD

Service Buffer = Service factor x Standard deviation

Replenishment Time = time for info to flow back + material processing time

Coefficient of Variation = $\dfrac{\text{Standard Deviation}}{\text{Mean or Average}}$

Risk Priority Number =   Severity x Occurrence x Detection

OEE =   Productivity x Availability x Yield

Change = $\underline{UN + V + CR + TPL}$
                                        $\qquad\quad R$
                                        Where UN = Understanding Need
                                        V = Vision, CR = current reality, TPL =
                                        Transition Plan and R = Resistance

Strategy Matrix

	1 Objective	2nd Objective	3rd Objective	4th Objective	5th Objective	6th Objective
Year 3						
Year 2						
Year 1						
TODAY						

Road Map

	Year 1				Year 2		Year 3	
	Q1	Q2	Q3	Q4	1st Half	2nd Half	1st Half	2nd Half
Objective 1								
Objective 2								
Objective 3								
Objective 4								
Objective 5								
Objective 6								

30, 60, 90 Day Plan

30 Days	60 Days	90 Days

Communications Plan

WHEN	WHAT	WHO	WHERE	NOTES
Daily				
Weekly				
Monthly				
Quarterly				

Endnotes

[i] <u>Webster's New World Dictionary of the American Language</u>. The Southwest Company: The World Publishing Company, Edition 1969.

[ii] <u>Webster's New International Dictionary Second Edition</u>. A Merriam-Webster: G. & C. Merriam Company, 1946.

[iii] ibid

[iv] isixsigma.com

[v] Taiichi Ohno June 1987

[vi] <u>Webster's New International Dictionary Second Edition</u>. A Merriam-Webster: G. & C. Merriam Company, 1946.

[vii] ibid

[viii] http://en.wikipedia.org/wiki/TAKT_time, 5/26/08

[1.] Taiichi Ohno, The Toyota Production System, Beyond Large Scale Production, English Translation Copyright 1988 at Productivity Press a Division of Kraus Productivity Organization Ltd.

[2.] Vision To Execution, Enduring Leadership Principles by 2004 by Marvin Covault

[3.] Hope is not a Method by Gordon Sullivan and Michael Harper, New York Broadway Books p 193

[4.] The National Training Center Matures by Anne Chapman 1993 TRADOC Historical Monograph

[5.] From Post-Mortem to Living Practice An in depth study of the evolution of the AAR by Marilyn Darling and Charles Parry 2000 by the Signet Consulting Group

For More Information
on
Ted Gee
and the services of SBI go to

strategicsolutionsbysbi.com

Printed in the United States
151675LV00001B/10/P